liberationmemories

African American Life Series

A complete listing of the books in this series can be found at the back of this volume.

Series Editors:

MELBA JOYCE BOYD

Department of Africana Studies,

Wayne State University

RON BROWN

Department of Political Science,

Wayne State University

liberationmemories
the Rhetoric and Poetics of
John Oliver Killens

KEITH GILYARD

Wayne State University Press   Detroit

07   06   05   04   03   5   4   3   2   1

Library of Congress Cataloging-in-Publication Data

Gilyard, Keith, 1952–
    Liberation memories : the rhetoric and poetics of John Oliver Killens / Keith
Gilyard.
        p. cm. — (African American life series)
    Includes bibliographical references (p.) and index.
    ISBN 0–8143-3057–6 ((cloth) : alk. paper)
    1. Killens, John Oliver, 1916—Criticism and interpretation.   2. Killens, John
Oliver, 1916—Aesthetics.   3. Killens, John Oliver, 1916—Technique.   4. African
Americans—Intellectual life.   5. African Americans in literature.   6. African
American aesthetics.   I. Title.   II. Series.
PS3561.I37 Z67 2003
813'.54—dc21   2002151897

toGrace

contents

acknowledgments

For their general support and encouragement, I thank a host of people too numerous to name here. I trust that they know my gratitude. For their specific assistance with the manuscript, I am greatly indebted to Alvin Aubert, Adam Banks, Bernard Bell, Melba Joyce Boyd, Deborah Breen, Clinton Crawford, Lita Cunningham, William Daly, Arthur Flowers, Kaamilah Gilyard, Beth Howse, Grace Killens, Kelly Malarky, Vorris Nunley, Yusuf Nuruddin, Howard Rambsy, Elaine Richardson, Evelyn Richardson, Lorenzo Thomas, and Vershawn Young.

In addition, I wish to thank the entire staffs of the National Baha'i Archives, the Medgar Evers College Library, and the Schomburg Center for Research in Black Culture.

introduction

On the night of March 22, 1986, septuagenarian John Oliver Killens made the last major public appearance of his career. He was received warmly by an admiring audience of hundreds who attended a dinner at Harvest Manor in Brooklyn, an affair held as part of the National Black Writers Conference. They showered appreciation upon a writer and activist who was the author of eight books, founding chairman of the legendary Harlem Writers Guild, a two-time nominee for the Pulitzer Prize, and a man regarded by some as the spiritual father of a generation of African-American novelists.[1] However, as the years pass and that buoyant occasion recedes further into the past, one is left to realize that despite the fact that Killens should be regarded as important, his literary reputation is far from secure. Much of his work is out of print. He has not been a popular subject for researchers. And although entries about him appear in several reference and critical works, he is not represented among the one hundred forty-nine selections discussed in *Masterpieces of African-American Literature* (1992). Nor is he among the more than one hundred writers included in the heralded *Norton Anthology of African American Literature* (1997) or among the dozens included in the *Prentice Hall Anthology of African American Literature* (2000).

His most notable African-American fiction-writing contemporaries, Ralph Ellison and James Baldwin, receive great attention and generate an abundance of ink. His fiction, viewed often as overly political or journalistic by detractors, fails to appeal to art-for-art's-sake advocates. Even those sympathetic to his message do not always embrace his technique. As Harish Chander observes relative to the fairly scant critical reception that does

1

exist, "appraisals of John Oliver Killens' fictional works that focus on his ideology and substance of his message have generally been positive, whereas those that focus on form and structure have generally been negative" (256).

Because no serious history of the development of the African-American novel from the 1950s onward can be constructed, as Addison Gayle and Bernard Bell have suggested, without considerable attention to Killens's contribution, we need a more informed and balanced critique that advances beyond the neglect of anthologists and the binarism indicated by Chander.[2] This book aims to support such a reckoning. The primary focus is an assessment of his novels from a rhetorical perspective. Rather than legitimizing the contention that so-called depoliticized writing is the cherished criterion that Killens's fiction fails to meet or the idea that technical blemishes in his work prevail, the governing premise here is that Killens's novels are best construed as tremendously artful renderings of African-American rhetorical forms and that the richest readings of his novels involve a knowledge of Black verbal traditions.

Killens was a novelist mainly concerned with articulating Black heroism, particularly within a family or community context, and offering a set of values he deemed liberatory. He often eschewed realism—assuming that by realism one means complex environmental and psychological portraiture—in favor of an insistence on noble and polemical characters. In his mission and view of art, he deliberately followed W. E. B. Du Bois, who, in a famous 1926 article titled "Criteria of Negro Art," wrote:

> All Art is propaganda and ever must be, despite the wailing of the purists. I stand in utter shamelessness and say that whatever art I have for writing has been used always for propaganda for gaining the right of black folk to love and enjoy. I do not care a damn for any art that is not used for propaganda. But I do care when propaganda is confined to one side while the other is stripped and silent. (296)

It must be noted that Du Bois was using *propaganda* in the more neutral sense the term conveyed, as Edward Corbett and Robert Connors remind us, before it took on "unfavorable connotations" (24–25). In addition, it must be stressed that the term *propaganda* for Du Bois did not imply any diminished artistry. He was merely affirming the persuasive aspect of art.

Killens was also a forerunner to Black Arts theorists like Larry Neal, who argued for the production of Black rhetorical art and the rejection of a Western critique.[3] For sure, only Black folks could put the "Black" in such art. On the other hand, to the extent that those critics meant "Western" to signify a uniform privileging by white critics of a restrictive formalism, they overstated their case. Wayne Booth, for example, had already effectively demonstrated the weakness and arbitrariness of the "pure art" position in his landmark book *The Rhetoric of Fiction*. Booth argued that any literary language that shows anything also serves to tell. He asserted that "the author cannot choose to avoid rhetoric; he can choose only the kind of rhetoric he will utilize. He cannot choose whether or not to affect his readers' evaluations by his choice of narrative manner; he can only choose whether to do it well or poorly" (149). Although certainly not flawless, the Killens fiction corpus represents a distinguished fusion of sociopolitical persuasion, or rhetoric, and literary artifact, or poetics.[4]

As I consider Killens's novels, individually or as a group, my investigation is organized sequentially, for the most part, in terms of three categories: vision, vehicle, and vernacular. This is similar to the taxonomy—theme, structure, saturation—that Stephen Henderson employed in the 1970s to examine the "new Black poetry," a poetry often viewed as parallel to Killens's fiction in the context of the Black Arts Movement. But while Henderson used *theme* to denote subject matter, I opt for *vision* because I want to emphasize that the writer is making an argument about a view of the world, not merely or neutrally trotting out provocative material for display. Thus my use of *vision* stretches Henderson's conceptualization of *theme*. On the other hand, by *vehicle* I mean something closely akin to what Henderson meant by *structure*, though I am more concerned with how the argument is articulated in rhetorical terms than I am in the genre elements typically associated with the novel. In other words, by *vehicle* I mean the most salient rhetorical devices used to carry the message. For the purposes of this inquiry, the primary topoi are the Black sermon; the elaborated folktale or epigraph; Du Bois's metaphors of the Talented Tenth, double consciousness, and the veil; literacy as emancipation; signifying, or humorous put-downs; the recurring image of Malcolm X; and the reinterpretation of community texts both sacred and secular. By *vernacular*, I mean the textual embellishments that derive from the linguistic, musical, folkloric, and religious practices of common African Americans. This is consonant with Henderson's notion of *saturation*, the detailed ways in which texts evince "Blackness." Or as Lumumba, narrator of *The Cotillion*, phrases the matter in the novel's foreword, "I decided to write my book in Afro-Americanese. Black rhythm, baby. Yeah, we got rhythm, brothers, sisters. Black idiom, Black nuances, Black style. Black truths. Black exaggerations" (6). Killens's use of the vernacular in *The Cotillion* and his other major novels will be detailed.

Incorporated into this book is examination of Killens's output as an essayist and cultural organizer. It helps to illumine his fiction; therefore, significant space is devoted to discussing those activities and the part they play in his overall message. More specifically, I am interested in the extent to which Killens's essays make up an African-American jeremiad, a major rhetorical form in the African-American intellectual tradition that expresses faith, unlike the tenets of the Black Arts Movement, that America's destiny is to become an authentic, pluralistic democracy. In addition, I demonstrate how the numerous conferences Killens organized serve as an elaborately constructed set of testimonials that endorse his views on cultural politics.

Chapter 1, then, deals with the major fictional statement that Killens made about the South, especially as related to heroic resistance, unity, and African-American folk wisdom. The relevant novels are *Youngblood* (1954) and *'Sippi* (1967). Chapter 2 re-

volves around *And Then We Heard the Thunder* (1962) and ex-
amines Killens's overall ideology and technique in more detail.
The appeals at the heart of *Black Man's Burden* (1965), his collection of essays, form the third chapter's core topic, although
significant references are made to several other Killens essays, to
his relationship with Malcolm X as evidenced by the charter of
the Organization of Afro-American Unity, and to the well-known
criticism of Killens contained in Harold Cruse's *Crisis of the Negro
Intellectual*. Chapter 4 considers *The Cotillion* (1971), perhaps the
most popular Killens novel, and how it reflects the Black cultural
revolution the author championed. Chapter 5 demonstrates how
Killens's call for a literature of Black heroes, myths, and legends
shapes *Slaves* (1969), *Great Gittin' Up Morning* (1972), *A Man
Ain't Nothin' but a Man: The Adventures of John Henry* (1975), and
the posthumously published *Great Black Russian: A Novel on the
Life and Times of Alexander Pushkin* (1989). Chapter 6 illustrates
how the various writers' conferences convened by Killens between
1965 and 1986 represent calculated amplifications of his voice.

Apparently Killens will always be associated with the Black
Arts Movement, and he should be. His challenging the "pure art"
position, his valorizing of African-American orality, and his creating idealized, heroic, and nationalist characters are hallmarks
of the Black Aesthetic. As such, his work remains relevant as
we continue to ponder the strengths and weaknesses of that aesthetic. Much of Killens's writing exists in dialogue with latter-day
critics like Deborah McDowell and Madhu Dubey. McDowell, in
"Boundaries: Or Distant Relations and Close Kin," claims that
the artistic formulas of the Black Arts Movement make race the
superordinate construct and thus engage in essentialism, subor-
dinating, for example, gender differences. Dubey is sympathetic
to McDowell's argument but also acknowledges, in *Black Women
Novelists and the Nationalist Aesthetic*, that the critical project of
the Black Aestheticians, particularly the debunking of art-for-
art's-sake rhetoric and the privileging of vernacular forms, both
ideas that were pushed strongly by Killens, made possible some
of the subsequent literary achievements of Black female writers.

This is undoubtedly a significant accomplishment of those theorists and practitioners. But although Killens's work should remain connected to deliberations about the Black Arts Movement, I argue for an even richer, more complex read. His ideas, as I hope to make clear, were more expansive and pluralistic than one might assume. I would even posit that Black nationalist writing by Killens is an example of what Gary Hatch describes as "community-based reasoning" (208–10). Using this technique, a rhetor does not forward the arguments most compelling to him or her if such arguments are not valued very highly by the community being addressed. Instead, reasoning is offered that aligns with the community's prevailing sentiments. This rhetorical move could be hypocritical—would be if the rhetor actually holds no belief in the propositions set forth—but it is not necessarily so. It is often like a witness telling the truth, indeed, maybe even nothing but the truth, but not the whole truth. As Hatch explains, "[T]he trick is to find reasons that the community will find persuasive and that you can accept and believe in" (209).

Before Killens, Langston Hughes engaged in a celebrated example of community-based reasoning. About to begin a reading tour in 1931 before mostly religious and somewhat conservative Black Southerners, Hughes realized that his recent poems reflecting a radical socialist aesthetic would not be received well. So he wrote poems for the tour like "The Negro Mother" to glorify Black culture and Black pride in a way that would appeal to his envisioned audience. Hughes, of course, was genuine in his celebration—but he also celebrated more.[5] In a similar fashion, Black nationalist writing does not represent the sum of Killens's ideology, even post-1960s. Such writing aims, rather, to persuade African-American readers to unite and perform the hard and difficult task of building adequate mechanisms of power. This is a mission in which Killens truly believed. As such, he understood that one cannot ignore appeals to Black nationalism and reasonably hope to capture the attention of the Black masses. However, the window of his provincialism always opened onto broader prospects of liberation.

Wanda Macon writes, in *The Oxford Companion to African American Literature*, that "Killens's name will forever ring simultaneously with the bells of freedom" (420). But for how many? I hope that whatever the current count, this book helps increase the numbers of readers and listeners.

chapter 1
SouthernExposure

A major aim of John Oliver Killens as a fiction writer was to present his understanding of Southern experience and to counsel African-American readers and others. This brand of deliberative discourse involved departures on two fronts. First, he had to dispel the rather significant myth that happy, contented "darkies" got along on the whole with their white counterparts in a perceived pastoral Southland. His fiction would refute that notion explicitly and repeatedly. Second, he chose to challenge the American tradition of fiction, even that of African Americans, and develop stories around positive and generative Black families, which he viewed as essential elements of the most important social gains that had been and could be achieved by the general African-American populace. In addition, Killens interpreted politics for his readers by activating his characters quite polemically. Thus his novels have been criticized for being too rhetorical, that is, overly concerned with persuasion. Of course, the point is moot for these purposes because the present goal is precisely to examine a fair sampling of his persuasive gestures, attempt to account for its construction, and contend that his rhetoric, rather than being perceived as a literary defect, is best construed as crucial to an impressive artistry. The texts highlighted in this chapter are the novels *Youngblood* and *'Sippi*, his most extensive representations of life and political activism in the South.

Published in 1954, *Youngblood* signaled a new direction for the African-American novel. Its title alone, a surname, besides suggesting new energy and insights, announces its difference from Black existential works like *Native Son* and *Invisible Man*. Killens rejects the overriding singular (son) presence in Wright's novel

9

and the isolated (man) absence in Ellison's. Particularly critical of *Invisible Man*, he wrote a harsh review in Paul Robeson's *Freedom* newspaper claiming that Ellison offered a commercial mix of sex, violence, red-baiting, and decadent African-American characters. He charged that Ellison portrays the incestuous Trueblood as representative of Black sharecroppers, that the veterans in the asylum are meant to symbolize the average Black soldier, that Rinehart typifies the Black pastor, and that the novel's protagonist is an Uncle Tom who kowtows to rich white people. Killens argued further that "this book would give the impression that the Negro people as a whole are a hopeless bunch of dehumanized beings. This is exactly the Big Lie that the enemies of Negro freedom have been telling the world since slavery time—that the Negro is subhuman" (7).

As indicated previously, Killens considered novels to be propaganda as well as art and was preoccupied with the idea that most African-American characters be cast in a positive light. Unfortunately, this view, admirable in many respects, seriously compromised his evaluation of *Invisible Man*. For one, Trueblood is not offered as the norm among Black farmers. He is an anomaly, a veritable outcast. A casual observer like Mr. Norton has to be guided to him. Likewise, the veterans are not presented as paradigmatic, nor is Rinehart intended to be illustrative of the African-American ministry in general. Furthermore, it is contradictory to assert that the protagonist is consumed by the desire to ascend the social ladder, which requires intelligence and talent in his case, while maintaining that Blacks are categorized as hopeless and subhuman, in other words, lacking intelligence. Despite these flaws in his reasoning, or indeed because of them, Killens pressed onward to the conclusion that *Invisible Man* constitutes a "vicious distortion of Negro life" and asserted further that the "Negro people need Ralph Ellison's *Invisible Man* like we need a hole in the head or a stab in the back" (7). Although the artistic differences between Killens and Ellison during the 1950s should not be understated, it must be noted that Ellison was a favorite target of the left, both Black and white, in

New York, who considered unflattering his depiction of leftist organizers.

The Killens viewpoint apparently prevailed inside the Harlem Writers Guild, of which Killens was the founding chairman. When *Youngblood* appeared, guild member John Henrik Clarke wrote in the August 1954 issue of *Freedom* that it was a story of "healthy Negroes" and called it "the best novel on Negro life that has appeared to date" (7). Killens would eventually soften his stance toward *Invisible Man*, and he even produced a Rinehart of his own nearly twenty years later in the satirical story "Rough Diamond." Nonetheless, the creation of positive Black characters remained his dominant concern.

Rather than portraying an individual's anguished quest for identity or self-fulfillment, Killens accepted an enabling Black identity as the rule, rather than the exception, and was driven to represent in *Youngblood* the heroic struggle of a family and community to persevere and thrive during the first third of the twentieth century. That Killens would perceive the family unit as the cornerstone of a successful mass confrontation with Jim Crow was predictable given the relative stability of his own upbringing. He shared a close bond, for instance, with his great-grandmother, Georgia Killens, whom he called Granny. She habitually regaled him with masterfully spun stories, which contained astute cultural criticism, often told as they walked the streets of Macon together. Although she died when Killens was five or six years old, she left behind plenty of material, much of it about her childhood years in slavery, that would show up in his work. She was, in fact, the model for Big Mama, the dominant figure in the early portion of *Youngblood*, whose forceful, deconstructive commentary infuses every scene. Echoing the wisdom dispensed by Granny, Big Mama refutes the idea that slaves felt there were benevolent masters worth serving. She remarks, "Crackers always talking about the slaves cried when Marster Lincoln sot us free. We cried all right, honey. Aah Lord—we cried. Won' a Negro's eyes dry that time. We cried for joy and shouted hallelujah" (6). This sentiment derives from that expressed by Granny, who informed young Killens, while criticizing a popular song about so-called mourning slaves, "Humph! Talking about 'All the darkies am aweeping.' We wept all right, honey bunch. We wept for joy and shouted halleluyah when Ol' Masser got the cold cold ground that was coming to him" ("The Half Ain't Never Been Told" 281).

Laurie Lee Barksdale, the central female character in the novel, benefits enormously from her grandmother's intellect and spirit. She is schooled by Big Mama always to resist oppression. Joe Youngblood, Laurie Lee's husband, is no less heroic. A dark and muscular six-foot-four, he goes to church on Sundays, sings bass in the glee club, and plays baseball on Saturday afternoons. Imagine Joe Louis, Josh Gibson, Paul Robeson, John Henry, and the most handsome and decent Baptist deacon ever all rolled into one. Having risked his life in Tennessee in an attempt to avoid being forced to perform involuntary labor on Mr. Buck's plantation, Joe has cut his teeth on struggle, though he somewhat regrets the solitary nature of his eventual escape, musing, "Shoulda brought some of them with me. . . . Shoulda talked them into it" (22).

After Laurie Lee and Joe marry, they settle in highly racialized Crossroads, Georgia, a metaphor for the Macon of Killens's youth and for a particular intersection. Pleasant Grove, the "colored section" of the town in which they live, is much like the Pleasant Hill community of real-life Macon. The Pleasant Grove School is the fictional counterpart to the Pleasant Hill School that Killens attended. The Youngblood children, Jenny Lee and Robby, were "born" around the same time as the author himself, Robby no doubt being a principal alter ego. With the idealized Youngblood family in place—mother, father, sister, brother—hardworking and virtuous, Killens has created his first major fictional vehicle to explore Black communal possibility within a social realm indelibly familiar to him.

The battle is pitched in both *Youngblood* and *'Sippi*; hardly a page goes by without Blackfolk having to resolve some crisis created by whites. Days upon days are wrapped in threat and death. Barely a conversation transpires without "boy," "sir," "nigrah," "cracker," "nigger," or "peckerwood." In the midst of these polarities, the author drives home the message that Black redemption can only come through Black unity. Building on solid foundations like the Youngblood family unit, the African-American community must construct an organized rebellion. Joe's favorite song, which functions as his (and the book's) mantra, is "Walk Together Children." Robby literally dreams of Black liberators:

> On one side was massed a great White army with ugly ghost-like faces, evil and leering. And on the other side the great Black army, proud and handsome and fierce and brave and everything else. And Mama was there and Daddy was there and Jenny Lee and Ben Raglin and Ida Mae Raglin and Fat Gus Mackey and everybody else. But most of all, Robby Youngblood was there, strong and mighty, leading the Black army to victory. (75–76)

Robby's dreams are commendable, but without manifest strength Blacks remain vulnerable in a hostile white environment, a lesson spelled out painfully for Robby in an episode drawn from an incident Killens experienced while a student at the segregated Pleasant Hill School, a dilapidated structure without running water and sufficient heat. On the way to and from classes, Killens and several of his schoolmates passed the colonial mansions of wealthy whites, often crossing paths with white children going to and from their own segregated school. One day at the crossroads (hence Crossroads, Georgia), a white student asked a friend of Killens, "Hey nigger, what you learn in school today?" The quick-witted boy replied, "I learned your mother was a whore." As the Black boys laughed in approval, the white boy became enraged and slapped the Black boy in the face, touching off a melee during which punches were thrown, rocks hurled, and sticks wielded. No one, however, was seriously injured, and the battle ended indecisively. Killens and his friends continued home, proud of their scrapes, bruises, and hard-won dignity. The next morning a squadron of police officers came to Pleasant Hill School and dragged several frightened Black children from the building. Not all of them had participated in the fight, and some who had been involved had been fortunate, like Killens, to be overlooked. No white children were apprehended. After the children were taken to the courthouse, their mothers were summoned and afforded a choice. Either they could beat their sons in front of the authorities as a lesson not to fight white kids, or they could watch their sons, none of whom was yet a teenager, be carted off to reform school. As much as the mothers hated to do it, every one of them whipped her son to save him from the reformatory (*Black Man's Burden* 102–5).

Nearly thirty years later, Killens retells the story in his first novel, with slight modifications, upping the dramatic ante. Robby, for instance, is not fighting merely because he won a quick game of insult; he had come to the rescue of Jenny Lee, who was being assaulted by a group of white boys while on her way home from school. Like the early Wright, Killens provides little moral wiggle room. Robby had been taught by his mother, following the lead of Big Mama, that his resistance was appropriate. Laurie Lee did not subscribe, as Wright's mother did, to the part of the "ethics of living Jim Crow" that banned fighting against white boys.[1] In her eyes, you fought whomever you had to fight to protect yourself and your loved ones. Regardless of the omnipresent danger for an assertive Black male, and remembering that her own brother Tim had been ruined by reform school after fighting white boys, she nonetheless refuses, as the saying goes, to shove Robby back into her womb. She concentrates instead on consciously grooming him to become a man unbowed and unwilling to be treated as socially inferior. That she inevitably acquiesces to authorities and beats Robby is a crushing defeat for her family, as it was for the real-life and nameless mothers. Laurie Lee made the right call, but the decision offers her no immediate solace.

Despite setbacks like the courthouse debacle, which almost tears apart the family because of the children's resentment and the parents' combination of anger and guilt, the Youngbloods, Robby especially, recapture the momentum toward Black community. As Robby thinks wistfully one day after a trip to the swimming hole with his friends, "If they kept being buddies even after they had become grown men and never stopped being buddies ever, then white folks wouldn't be able to touch them with a ten-foot pole" (110). Robby also is the catalyst for resolving tensions between African Americans in the South and those from the North. Such divisiveness, ridiculous to Killens, who basically viewed the whole nation as Southern, stifles a valuable exchange of perspectives and impedes the development of the strongest possible African-American community in Crossroads and beyond.[2] So when Robby's friends disparage the idea of having a teacher from up North, even before they have met him, it is Robby who exhorts them to lay aside their prejudices and give the new teacher a chance. The children are rewarded immeasurably when the teacher, Richard Wendell Myles, brings to town a much needed and ultimately appreciated radicalism. As Frederick Douglass wrote, as Mr. Myles remembers from college, and as Killens himself quoted countless times during his own public career: "If there is no struggle there is no progress. Those who profess to favor freedom, and yet depreciate agitation, are men who want crops without plowing the ground. They want rain without thunder and lightning. They want the ocean without the awful roar of its many waters" (*Youngblood* 136).[3]

Killens's father was Charles Myles Killens; thus he is the source of the fictional teacher's surname as well as one of the sources of his spirit. The author recalls with awe and fondness an incident that occurred in Macon in 1932 when his father managed a restaurant in the Black business district and sixteen-year-old Killens worked behind the counter. Two white men entered and one, who was apparently inebriated, demanded to be served. The elder Killens informed the man that it was against the law to serve him and declined. The man would not go easily or quietly; in fact, he became quite aggressive, creating a tense situation that was finally resolved when the elder Killens brandished a pistol. Young John was proud yet fearful, understanding that "Black manhood and Black womanhood were hazardous pursuits, inflationarily expensive" ("The Half Ain't Never Been Told" 283–84).

The Mr. Myles of *Youngblood* also derives, as Stephen Carey suggests, from the concept of the Talented Tenth. As he comments on Killens's characters generally: "In the social arenas of education, religion and politics, Killens develops heroic leadership as highly educated, as directly interested in the 'uplift' of the common masses, and as intensely active in directly resisting racial oppression. His protagonists must meet Du Boisian standards. Killens is particularly interested in developing heroes who serve as the Talented Tenth for the Black southern underclass" (2–3). Of course, Du Bois popularized the notion of the Talented Tenth in the early twentieth century, the idea being that the best among African Americans—the most capable, gifted, promising, and highly educated sector or "tenth"—would save the ethnic group as a whole from the worst social ravages. Not only did Du Bois posit that such aristocratic leadership eventually would be successful, he argued that it was the quickest way to effect the social uplift of the African-American masses. However, he later expanded and revised his thinking largely because, in his own view, he had failed to emphasize the importance of self-sacrifice in his initial conception. The Talented Tenth often operated more in its own interests than on behalf of the group. Du Bois also developed an appreciation for mass organization, activity he felt should be guided by socialist principles.[4] In any event, Killens, for whom Du Bois was a personal and invaluable mentor, was enormously influenced by Du Bois's more mature version of the Talented Tenth.[5] Thus the "Du Boisian standards" Carey references emanate, for Killens, from Du Bois's latter convictions as expressed in the 1948 "Talented Tenth Memorial Address."

The Du Boisian Mr. Myles has an immediate impact on Robby Youngblood. After learning in school about Harriet Tubman and the Underground Railroad, Robby has another dream: "Laurie Lee Youngblood was the conductor and Robert Youngblood was the engineer, and the train was long and black and beautiful, like the Mary Jane Special, but longer and blacker and even more beautiful. And black folks got on at every stop—Everybody headed for that thing called Freedom" (158).

Mr. Myles also presents his brand of activism to Laurie Lee and Joe, who have been rebels, at least in spirit, all along. Joe Young-blood is intrigued by how Mr. Myles's "book learning" essentially restates Joe's own heartfelt impulses. Joe understands that "We got to fight . . . *We?*—*We?* Yes . . . —*We*—We—You mighty right—*We*—We—We got to band together and fight— . . . We got to get together and fight these peckerwoods down to the ground" (203). Immediately thereafter, this idea is tested as Joe's paymaster at the mill continues his practice of shorting Joe on his pay. When Joe takes umbrage and successfully demands a proper account-ing, he is supported by three of his African-American coworkers. As the four of them leave the mill, Joe feels that the combined strength of the others actually enters his body (211). While he strolls amid the African-American crowd on Harlem Avenue on his way to the barbershop, he is keenly aware—having been made hyperperceptive by the incident at the mill and his accompanying nervousness—of the Black throng's productive capability if they would only, as his most cherished song advises, walk together.

Laurie Lee, actually quicker to action than her husband is and who may be the stronger character, exclaims after hearing of the mill incident and the response of the three coworkers, "When a Negro's in trouble with the white man it's every Negro's business" (223). One recalls the fervent, community-spirited rhetoric—"injustice anywhere is a threat to justice everywhere"—later ex-pressed by Martin Luther King, Jr., in his "Letter from Birming-ham Jail."[6]

As necessary as an activist Black solidarity is, it is not sufficient to revamp relations in the South in line with Killens's vision. His outlook required a coalition of revolutionary African Americans and progressive European Americans to address fully economic exploitation, a matter that was at least as important to Killens as civil rights. This inclination on his part is traceable, Du Bois aside, to his involvement in the labor movement. He was the first African American on the staff of the National Labor Relations Board, where he worked from 1936 to 1942 and again briefly af-ter World War II. He was also an organizer for the Congress of

Industrial Organizations, founded in 1938 under the direction of John L. Lewis, president of the United Mine Workers of America. His multiethnic vision may also have stemmed from his experiences at the Ballard Normal School, which he attended from the eighth grade until his graduation from high school. Established by the Congregational Church and the American Missionary Association, Ballard had an ethnically diverse faculty, which was very unusual in the Deep South. Most of the white teachers hailed from New England or out West and were considered pariahs by most white Maconites. One teacher, an Iowan named Lewis H. Mounts, impressed on Killens the need to be available for social service ("The Half Ain't Never Been Told" 284). Killens already felt this way, at least to some degree, because of his upbringing, but Mounts felt the idea could never be emphasized enough. Mounts was respected and genuinely liked by the African-American community in Macon and survives, in part, in Oscar Jefferson, the white character in *Youngblood* who most symbolizes the role that whites should play in the struggle according to Killens. Oscar, suspected by his own kind of being a "nigger lover," is the answer to the wry question Joe Youngblood had posed while listening to Mr. Myles: "Where the white friends at?" (204).

Having formed, or at least hinted at, his core coalition in the first half of the novel—rock-solid African-American Southern family, Northern Black intellectual, the heretofore underachieving Black masses, the white working class—Killens puts the group through its paces during the second half by exposing them to progressively more difficult challenges, prepping them for a final test of empowerment. One major battle concerns the rhetoric of Jubilee, an annual concert of Negro spirituals presented, grudgingly, by the students of Pleasant Grove School. The students resent singing for the amusement of a largely white audience and feel betrayed when Mr. Myles, whom they thought might resist, agrees to coordinate the show. However, Mr. Myles, inspired by Reverend Ledbetter, develops a twist, incorporating into Jubilee a narrative explaining the messages of rebellion encoded in the spirituals. The narrator, Robby Youngblood, would explain, therefore, that

"Swing Low Sweet Chariot" and "Steal Away to Jesus" allude to escape via the Underground Railroad and that "Go Down, Moses" celebrates Harriet Tubman. For Myles and Ledbetter it is a question of unity and responsibility. As the reverend declares, "They will be singing for our fathers and our fathers' fathers back through the ages and for generations to come" (272).

Another comparison with King is instructive. As Keith Miller indicates in "Martin Luther King, Jr. Borrows a Revolution," "one of King's foremost rhetorical strategies was to locate his appeal within the context of cherished religious, cultural, and patriotic traditions" (249). This is exactly the stratagem Killens employs, using the highly valued spirituals, especially when explicated his way, as a mechanism of empathy, accessing a cosmology shared by the Black community of Crossroads and by much of his envisioned audience. Although Killens was not particularly religious, he knew his people were, so he prodded them to be simultaneously religious and revolutionary. He saw the "Sorrow Songs" as a ready medium.[7] As he recalls:

> I believe that those spirituals, like I said in one of those
> sections dealing with the spirituals, that the spirituals was
> a means for black people to organize themselves against
> slavery. I know that a lot of people I—I had a debate with
> a black woman singer, who said that I was reading some
> things into Negro spirituals that [only] do just what they seem
> to be, a childlike manifestation of black people, and their
> childlike belief in God, etc.—, I always thought the spirituals
> to be much more than that. . . . All of the insurrections
> were planned in the church. (Interview with Paul Lehman
> included in Lehman 148–50)[8]

The reconstituted Jubilee is a huge hit with the African-American audience and Oscar Jefferson. In disgust, many of the whites leave midway through the program. This disgruntled group could have obtained the dismissal of Mr. Myles if his support from the Black community had not been so strong.

A second formidable task facing the coalition is to organize a hotel workers union at the Oglethorpe Hotel, where Rob Young-blood, now a young man, holds a job as a bellhop, work that Killens himself performed in Macon while in high school. As the Great Depression sets in, Black workers are afraid to make waves and risk what meager jobs they have. White workers prefer to accept unfit work conditions rather than cast their lot with Blacks. They are willing to endure exploitation and work against their own economic interests as long as they can retain white privilege. Of course, the ethnic split among the labor force only serves the owners.

Killens had observed firsthand that white working-class racists were the major impediment to the labor movement in the South, a region whose workers were among the most victimized in the nation. Having been both a non-union worker and, subsequently, a labor organizer engaged in CIO endeavors in the South in the 1940s, a movement known as Operation Dixie, he bore witness that racialized identities were more important than class affiliation to many whites. They preferred segregated misery to integrated unions. As he later wrote in *Black Man's Burden:*

> When "Operation Dixie" invaded the South, Negroes hailed
> it as the Freedom Train, and they leaped aboard with great
> enthusiasm and profound dedication. But the train got bogged
> down very quickly and finally was derailed in the muck and
> mire of white supremacy. . . . The CIO's "Operation Dixie,"
> like reconstruction, indeed like the American Revolution
> and every other movement that should have spelled freedom
> and equality for Americans of all colors and religions, died
> stillborn. To give the C.I.O. its due, it did not keep the
> Negroes *out.* The trouble was that it could not keep the white
> workers *in.* (62)

The task of galvanizing the support of white hotel workers falls to Oscar Jefferson, who manages to convince a few that an integrated union beats none at all. Rob Youngblood emerges as the central figure of Black unionizing activity. African-American workers are skeptical of eventually joining forces with whites, as Rob urges, but eventually realize they have no better choice. As Willabelle Braxton reasons, "If we don't use the crackers against Mr. Ogle, Mr. Ogle'll use them against us" (404).

During the labor movement section of *Youngblood*, Killens mischievously "enters" his own text—sort of like a Hitchcock cameo—a maneuver he would later repeat in *The Cotillion*.[9] As organizer Jim Collins, formerly known as Jim Kilgrow, returns to Crossroads after a long absence to promote union activity, Oscar Jefferson, who had been a childhood friend, recognizes him during a meeting:

> "Excuse me folks," Oscar said, "It's been such a long time since I seen this boy."
> "Boy?" Jim Collins said.
> "Mr. Kil—I mean Mr. Collins."
> "That's more like it," Jim said. He turned to the others.
> "Well let's get down to the case on the docket." (402–3)

The ultimate question for the Killens coalition is whether it will hang together and defend itself in the face of violent onslaught. After Joe Youngblood is gunned down during a second pay dispute at the mill, the Black community proves more than willing, chasing the Ku Klux Klan from Rockingham Quarters with volleys of bullets. Although Joe will no longer walk among them, they will still walk together. Robby's foreshadowing dreams reach fruition in some form. Laurie Lee and Jenny Lee stand majestic. Mr. Myles performs heroically in an attempt to save Joe's life, and Oscar Jefferson's son, whose blood type, unlike most of the African Americans tested, matches Joe's, contributes to a transfusion as Killens symbolizes the shortcomings of a purely racialized vision and further expresses his optimism about youth.

Joe Youngblood wonders how he is supposed to live in the white man's world. The answer from Killens is that Black people can only begin to live meaningfully when they live in harmony

with one another and adopt a posture of self-defense. Killens had
always been reminded that such action was needed. When he was
participating in a discussion group as a college student in Atlanta
during the 1935–36 academic year, a white student announced
that he had the answer to the racial problem in the United States.
As his audience tensely awaited his pronouncement, he declared
that the "'nigrah' problem could be solved by drowning all the
'nigrahs' in the river" (*Black Man's Burden* 79–81).

    'Sippi, published in 1967, begins in fictional time, June 1954,
the same month *Youngblood* was actually released. The novel
is virtually a sequel; in fact, some of the material in the latter
story is drawn from the nearly two hundred pages that Killens
trimmed from the original manuscript of *Youngblood* at the request of his publishers, who thought the one-thousand-page draft
unwieldy.[10] Black solidarity and resistance are once again central
themes. The characters lack the near-perfect nobility of those
in the earlier book, which makes them somewhat more realistic.
Notwithstanding, Charles (Chuck) Othello Chaney, the most important figure, is yet a close approximation of Rob Youngblood.
His parents share most traits with the elder Youngbloods. Cora
Mae, Bessie Mae, Little Jake Carson, Reverend Purdy, Phil Ja-
cobson, and David Woodson correspond rather neatly to Willabelle, Ida Mae, Fat Gus Mackey, Reverend Ledbetter, Richard
Myles, and Jim Collins. Carrie Louise Wakefield serves as the
token, albeit embattled, white sympathizer. The working-class
African-American community in Minksville is analogous to the
one in Pleasant Grove, and a poorer community in the Bottom
is similar to the one in Rockingham Quarters. As for setting,
Wakefield County, Mississippi, of the 1950s and 1960s is every bit as racially segregated and harsh as Cross County, Georgia, of the 1920s and 1930s—if not more so—which is why this
rendition of the Killens coalition, a sort of Dream Team II, is
assembled.

    Additionally, Killens unveils variations of several set pieces
used previously. The image of the "Big Black Burly Negro that ran
amuck," part of a radio account of the Joe Youngblood shooting

(443), becomes, in *'Sippi*, a newspaper boy's shout of "Extra! Extra! BIG BURLY NEGROES RUN AMOK!" as two of the Chaney sons are on the lam after a confrontation with a white department store salesman (34). Chuck Othello consumes too much ice cream and becomes sick just as Jenny Lee Youngblood gorges herself with birthday cake and falls ill. Both actions are responses to chronic deprivation. Young Chuck Othello shares Robby Youngblood's habit of dreaming about social progress for African Americans, writing out his fantasies on occasion:

> My home is my house and my land is my land and my country
> is my country, even though it is not really my home, or my land,
> or my country. Yet it must be. And I must make it be. All by
> myself and single-handed, if it's got to be that way. I will be a black
> knight on a black horse in a black and shining armor. I will be
> John Henry, Robin Hood, and Joe Louis and Paul Robeson and
> Abraham Lincoln and Matt Dillon and Jackie Robinson and Jesse
> Chaney Junior all rolled into one. And I will make the land my
> land. Our land. (82–83)

Killens even invokes the title of the earlier work when Bessie Mae writes to Chuck Othello, who is by then away at college, and conveys her wish that he were back home being active in local political affairs. "They needed *young blood*, especially with an education, to lead the struggle" (209, emphasis mine).

The primary difference in the "teams'" missions in the two novels lies in the specific nature of Black political engagement. Whereas in *Youngblood* the focus is on the founding of an NAACP branch and the development of a labor union, the major objective in *'Sippi* is to seize political power through the ballot and even up the body count between the African-American community and white supremacists. Writer David Woodson and Reverend Purdy provide the most compelling oratory for voter registration and aggressive political action. Purdy preaches *the* classic sermon in African-American literature, a moving message of freedom and unity delivered in the Black vernacular. For example:

Douglass and Tubman and Turner was they brother's keeper.
Yes they was. When they theyselfs got free, they didn't stop
fighting like you woulda done. They dedicated they lives to
the freedom of they black brothers and sisters! . . . Running
around here talking about it's a free country and talking about
you a citizen, and yet you scared to go down to the courthouse
and register to vote. Well, you a lie and the truth ain't in
you. . . . Talking about you tryna make a better life for your
childrens yet you scared to do a little old thing like register to
vote. You a lie and the truth ain't in you! . . . And when you
don't vote . . . you cheating your children and your children's
childrens. And cheating is ugly and God A'mighty sure don't
love ugly. . . . Are you ready for the little black train? . . . Are
you ready for the freedom train? That's the train I'm talking
about this evening. (150–51)

During the course of the novel, Reverend Purdy assumes a heroic
stance reminiscent of the role models he mentions.

Of course, a similar burden must be shouldered by anyone bear-
ing the name Othello, a tribute to Paul Robeson and his legendary
portrayal of the Shakespearean character. By Killens's own account, Robeson was the most significant male influence in his life
next to his father. A large poster of Robeson hung in the Killens
home.[11]

The Chaney surname invokes civil rights martyr James Chaney,
and the first half of 'Sippi is testimony to the worth of the civil
rights movement. The latter half is a call for Black Power. And
Killens keeps the action hot indeed; the temperature is symboli-
cally kept above one hundred degrees for virtually all of the final
two hundred pages. White supremacists have made it clear, particularly by the bombing murder of registration activist Luke Gibson
and his family, that violence is the language they best speak. This
is standard fare in Black protest writing. However, Killens provides a vision of the South in the 1960s that includes many white
casualties as well when a veritable war erupts in Wakefield County
after the assassination of Woodson. Killens articulates vividly that

sufficient social redress cannot be accomplished by passive means. As Chuck Othello explains to Mr. Wakefield, in phrasing the author himself would later employ in numerous speeches, "Rocking the boat—why should we black folk be worried about rocking the goddamn boat, when we're not even in the boat, but drowning in the open sea? Our job is to capsize the boat—and build another one with accommodations for everybody" (399).[12]

At the close of 'Sippi, which, like Youngblood, concludes with the death of an African-American male hero and the promise of heightened political involvement by the African-American community, Killens elaborately reorchestrates the optimism that inflects the final passages of Youngblood, this time listing organizations that will effect political change instead of mentioning individuals:

> Came from SNCC, from SCLC, NAACP, the Urban League,
> CORE, NNLC, came from the Council of Negro Women,
> from the Federation of Colored Women's Clubs. The Muslims
> and Christians came. Jews came. Even infidels. The Deacons
> and the Elders came with their arms and ammunition. Men
> came from the labor movement. Came from the Willing
> Workers Club of Harlem, the Busy Bees, the Shining
> Lights, the Yorubas, the Climbers, the Ebonites, the Elks,
> the Masons. (433)

Although generally considered more nationalist by the late 1960s, Killens offers a view at the conclusion of 'Sippi that, given the political postures of some of the groups mentioned, suggests multiple possibilities for struggle. While it is true that Carrie Louise Wakefield, the last prominent European American character in Killens's fiction, is in effect banished from the African-American side of the civil rights movement by Charles Othello Chaney, a sharp contrast to the fact that Oscar Jefferson sits on the executive committee of the hotel workers union chaired by Rob Youngblood, it is also the case that Killens remained true to the idea of progressive pluralism or radical democracy. He was simply not interested much in, say, lunch-counter integration and felt that the most important function for white activists was to educate and organize members of the white community.

Youngblood and *'Sippi* make up a one-man Southern reconstruction. Killens consciously intended, as he points out in the introduction to the anthology *Black Southern Voices*, which appeared posthumously, to help build a Black Southern literary tradition distinct from, and in large measure oppositional to, that produced by the likes of Eudora Welty and William Faulkner, a body of work Killens terms "an apologia for the status quo" (2). Indeed, an examination of Welty's *One Writer's Beginnings* reveals no concern on her part with racist oppression in Jackson, Mississippi, where she grew up on the right (white) side of the tracks. From the other side hailed an African-American boy only seven months her senior who would also become known in literary circles, one Richard Nathaniel Wright. Concerning Faulkner, Killens satirizes him in *'Sippi*, using Mr. Wakefield as a mouthpiece: "Willie Faulkner was a friend of mine. He used to visit at the other house. All I'm saying is what he advocated. Take it easy right along in here, or else even if you win there'll be bitterness for centuries" (396). When such logic fails to persuade Charles Othello Chaney to abandon his belief in the ideology of Black Power, not to mention its exigence, Wakefield issues a blunt warning: "Don't fool yourself, boy. Willie Faulkner was right. My own Negroes will join up with me and kill other Negroes. All I got to say is, 'Come on boys, pick up your guns and follow me'" (399).[13]

Although Killens's fiction is obviously didactic, it is also immensely artful. With magnificent skill he melds key elements of the African-American rhetorical tradition into tales of dramatic force. This is not to say one should not criticize Killens's prose on the grounds that his work is sometimes too repetitious, overly journalistic, or less subtle than it could be. These are the familiar complaints. But to render the most informed judgment on style and structure, one needs to be familiar with, to invoke Geneva Smitherman, the "Black modes of discourse" on which Killens drew.[14] *Youngblood*, for example, is an African-American sermon in the form of a novel. '*Sippi* is a complex, recursive rewriting of an African-American folktale. All other textual aspects of the novels—inclusion of spirituals, biographical material, the Talented Tenth trope—connect within the context of these two basic structures.

Paul Lehman recognizes the secular Black sermon that is part and parcel of *Youngblood*. Each of the novel's four sections begins with a title and an excerpt from a Negro spiritual. Part 1, titled "In the Beginning," begins with "Didn't my Lord deliver Daniel/And why not every man?" Part 2, "No Hiding Place," starts with "I went to the rock to hide my face/The rock cried out—No hiding place." Part 3, "Jubilee," opens with "One of these mornings about five o'clock/This old world's gonna reel and rock/Pharoah's Army got drowned." The last part, "The Beginning," commences with "And before I'd be a slave/I'd be buried in my grave/And go home to my Lord/And be free." Each pair of title and excerpt marks discursive boundaries relative to an overarching story of Black awareness, Black commitment, Black organization, and Black rebellion. Inside the identified subject, African-American history and culture are the preacher's texts. The aforementioned spirituals, for example, are used as opposed to the Bible. In this context, the activist Reverend Ledbetter is a deliverer of condensed sermons inside the master sermon delivered by Killens. At one point, Lehman extracts *Youngblood* from its literary genre by claiming that "*Youngblood* is not a novel; it is a black sermon" (52). There is no need to concede that much territory to formalists, and Lehman does later reclaim some turf. *Youngblood* is indeed a novel, but a Black sermonic one replete with an elaborate "call" to which it is hoped that readers "respond." Part of the call involves numerous examples of narrative sequencing, or the forwarding of stories, as Smitherman explains, to make a case. As she writes:

> The relating of events (real or hypothetical) becomes a black rhetorical strategy to explain a point, to persuade holders of opposing views to one's own point of view, and in general to "win friends and influence people." This meandering away

from the "point" takes the listener on episodic journeys and over tributary routes, but like the flow of nature's rivers and streams, it all eventually leads back to the source. Though highly applauded by blacks, this narrative linguistic style is exasperating to whites who wish you'd be direct and hurry up and get to the point. (*Talkin and Testifyin* 147–48)

In the case of *Youngblood*, the "call" consists of numerous episodes, literally spanning hundreds of pages, about pride, self-determination, and self-defense designed to inspire readers to action.

Although *'Sippi*, like *Youngblood*, contains sermonic elements, the outstanding formal characteristic of *'Sippi* is that it essentially and intricately revolves around a single folktale. Lehman does not know the tale, "'Sippi," which is why, trying to account for the book's structural departure from *Youngblood*, he reasons that "this sermon follows one basic text" (61). But the sermon model does not yield the best description of *'Sippi*'s design. On the other hand, William Wiggins, Jr., who has written the most extensive and insightful analysis of *'Sippi*, notes:

Killens has made the customary literary use of this folklore genre; he uses them, that is, to invoke some response from his readers, such as humor or social protest. In many of his folktales humor and social protest are combined. In *'Sippi* he not only uses the message of the traditional folklore genre, but more importantly, he uses the structure of the folktale as a formal outline for his novel. Hence, it is not possible to remove the "'Sippi" folktale from Killens novel and have the same book: the novel *'Sippi* is a bigger and much more sophisticated offspring of her folktale father. (100)

The story Wiggins refers to was popular in the 1960s. He heard the version below from Reverend J. L. Parks of Louisville, Kentucky:

Negroes getting mean now. They ain't taking no more stuff off the white man. Like this mad Negro who went up to these

white folks that he's worked for all his life and said, "Ain't
gon be no more Mister Charlie. It's just Charlie from now
on." Then he looked at his wife and said, "Ain't no more Miss
Ann. It's just plain Ann from now on." After saying this the
Negro turned in a huff to leave. But when he got to the door
he turned again and said, "And another thing! Ain't no more
Mississippi! It's just plain 'Sippi from now on!" (101)

The mood of African-American rebellion that was in the air is
symbolized by a man who will reject Southern custom, challenge
the privilege and status of the white man, then the white woman,
and fearlessly express total rejection of the overall structure of
white supremacy.

Killens amplifies this folktale in 'Sippi's prologue. Jesse Chaney,
who hears the news regarding Brown v. Board of Education, dashes
from the cotton field to the home of Charles James Richard Wakefield, the biggest Mr. Charlie in the county. The following quote
indicates in detail how Killens uses his gift for satire to expand on
the common tale:

> As Jesse came within about a hundred yards of the Big House,
> Wakefield broke into a great big smile of friendly welcome.
> Jesse's mere presence always gave him a genuine warm feeling
> of one human being to another, the kind of feeling that did
> not come easily these days. It also gave him a feeling of the
> rightness of his approach to his Negroes. But now the smile
> left his face, unknowingly, as he watched Jesse continue
> toward the front porch where he stood beneath the electric
> fan. Instead of his flanking movement to go around to the
> back door, old Jesse came straight across the yard. In the
> entire relationship between these lifelong friends, Jesse had
> never before come straight across the front yard. Never ever.
> Wakefield did not want to believe what his eyes beheld.
> But by the time Jesse was ten or fifteen feet away from the
> porch, it became obvious, even to a friend like Wakefield,
> that this particular day was different from all the other days

in the world. And Jesse was not going to stand on tradition or
formality. Wakefield was afflicted with lockjaw, momentarily.
As Jesse kept coming toward the porch, he ultimately found
his voice again.

He was more flabbergasted than angry with his boyhood
friend. "What's the matter with you, Jesse boy? The heat got
the best of you?"

"The Supreme Court done spoke!" Jesse shouted, like
he had just got that old time religion and his soul had been
converted. "Ain't going around to the back door no more.
Coming right up to the front door from now on!"

"What'd you say?" Wakefield asked him, thinking maybe
he had not heard properly. It was too hot to get angry with
the best friend he had in all the world. Jesse was humility
personified. Yet and still—

"And another thing—ain't no more calling you Mister
Charlie. You just Charles from here on in. Or Jimmy Dick."

Wakefield's face lost color. The fan blew heat onto his
forehead now. "Jesse, you going too damn—"

Jesse turned to saintly Anne Barkley Wakefield who
wouldn't harm a mosquito if it were biting the tip of her
turned-up nose. "And another thing—no more calling you
Missy Anne. You just plain old common Annie from now
on."

The sweet angelic woman gasped and put her handkerchief
to her mouth. She stopped rocking momentarily. Her world
was moving swiftly out from under her. This was too much for
Charles Wakefield. Friendship or no friendship. Wakefield was
completely out of control, a thing that seldom happened to
him. Sweet and painful years of racial understanding and race
philosophizing went by the everlasting boards. Even as he told
himself, "Keep calm, C. J. R. Wakefield," almost against his
will he heard himself shout:

"Nigger, don't you know you're in Mississippi?"

Wakefield immediately wished he could call the words
back but they were gone from him forever. He had not

meant to call his close friend, "nigger." Yet he felt a kind
of cleansing of his heart and soul. He felt whiter, purer, inside.
The atmosphere was clearer now. And he was somehow glad
he had brought things out in the open, things that had been
hidden between them all these many years. Sometimes the
"word" had to be used to put things in perspective. Even
between the best of friends. It had a therapeutic value for
everyone concerned. Jesse would bow his humble head now,
ever so slightly, and hide the hurt in his eyes with the noble
savage's smile of profound humility. He would put his tail
between his legs and go around to the back door, and God
would be up in His Heaven again and all would be right with
the world. Wakefield would forgive and forget. He was the
biggest man in Mississippi. He could afford to be forgiving.

Obviously, Jesse had not read the script. "That's another
thing," the noble savage shouted, like he was preaching
from a colored Hardshell Baptist pulpit. "Ain' no more
Mississippi. Ain' no more Mississippi. It's jes' 'Sippi from
now on!" (xviii–xix)

As one can see, Killens is totally faithful to the basic import of
the folktale while at the same time embellishing the story to
account for character, extended dialogue, and reaction, as well
as to establish the specific social and historical context.

Wiggins identifies eleven cycles in *'Sippi*, ascending from lesser
to greater significance, that reflect the four-part motif of the
"'Sippi" folktale. For example, Jesse Chaney's early insistence on
manhood for himself and Chuck Othello eventually evolves into
Othello's militant confrontation with Wakefield and Woodson's
uncompromising call for Black empowerment. Single acts of Black
defiance lead to mass Black defiance. Young Chuck Othello's innocent game of house with Carrie Wakefield is enlarged, when he
later sleeps with her, into the adult flouting of a sexual taboo. Un-
publicized repercussions for bucking the political order give way
to ramifications that are tragic and epic in scope. The novel thus
builds to its conclusion through a series of repetitive anecdotes

within the thematic constraints of the "'Sippi" folktale. This gives
the book an African-American oral quality because, as commonly
noted, a hallmark of African-American storytelling, indeed of
African art forms in general, is a series of "rising" repetitions often accompanied by insertions of self-reflective summarizing, or
what is termed parallel phrasing. In addition, there is another
rhetorical feature, known as parataxis (the creation of a string
of statements that exist as interchangeable wholes within a fluid
matrix), that Wiggins has cited as operative in 'Sippi.[15] For example, there is an episode in which Jesse Chaney's cow is missing.
He suspects that it has been taken by someone on the Wakefield
plantation, but he is hesitant to reclaim it, only doing so after
his manhood is challenged by his wife. The cow, Missy Anne,
is alluded to several times later in the tale. The "Missy Anne"
references are not, however, tightly bound to the story line, nor
do they contribute to dramatic action; they seem, instead, sort
of floating signifiers that emphasize the reduction of the status
of "Miss Anne" to unremarkable—no more noteworthy than a
cow—in the mind of the Black man. This particular, free-floating
aspect of parataxis, associated with groups in West Africa, has
been manifest in African-American ballads and the blues, and
now hip-hop ("throw your hands up in the air"), where certain
cherished stanzas or classic lines are repeated in a wide variety
of songs.[16]

The lengthy, cyclical quality of *Youngblood* and *'Sippi* directly
stems from Killens's adherence to the requirements of the African-
American oral forms with which he experiments. His desire to
reflect Black experience in this manner and his aim to capture the
rhythms and nuances of the Southern folk characters who make
up the bulk of his cast would not lead to the lean, sparse, densely
symbolic novels that some critics prefer but to chanty, preachy,
folkloric, elaborately oral ones.

Bound up with political vision and major tropes is a series of
stylistic flourishes drawn from African-American culture. Killens
writes much of his dialogue, as epitomized by Purdy's sermon, in
Black Vernacular English, even commenting on his use of this

language variety along the way. As Charles Chaney muses in *'Sippi* during a voter registration drive:

> He wondered why so many black folk preferred to call it
> "reddishing" instead of registration. He'd heard so many
> Negroes in the county say, and proudly, "I'm gon reddish if
> it's the last damn thing I do before I die." He'd heard others
> say, "I ain't studying about that reddishing mess." Did he
> say "reddish" before he entered the University? Maybe
> it was a sarcastic joke his folk played deliberately on the
> English language. They sure didn't owe the English language
> anything. It had been used against them ever since they were
> brought here to this place. (372)

Similarly, in *Youngblood*, Laurie Lee initially tends to "correct" Joe's English, causing him to withdraw from conversation. But she soon comes to appreciate his "unaffected dignity" and "mother-wit that no amount of education could take the place of" (26).

Robby receives early and important exposure to the game of insult known as the dozens when he witnesses an exchange between Fat Gus Mackey and Sonny Boy. Fat Gus initiates the verbal sparring by dismissing the "No Trespassing" sign on Mr. Rayburn's property:

> "To hell with Cracker Rayburn. I had Mizzes Cracker last
> night. She didn't say *No Trespassing*."
> . . . Sonny Boy looked at Gus and said, "Now aintchoo
> something? Boy I bet you wouldn't know what to do with it if
> Old Lady Cracker offered it to you. Be so sked you wouldn't
> know what to do."
> "Your dear-rold mother didn't say that last night. She
> didn't say I didn't know what to do."
> Sonny Boy eyed Gus, made his face look serious. "Look out
> boy," he said good-naturedly. "You better watch that stuff. You
> know goddamn well I don't play no dozens." He picked up a
> rock.

"Pat your damn feet then," Fat Gus told him. "Louis Armstrong plays it." All the boys laughed. (105)

Robby's immersion into this speech circle and, by extension, the broader African-American community enables the camaraderie that comes to inform his activism.

Killens also reworks standard phrasings to create Black semantics, which he uses to promote images of African-American beauty and dignity. For example, when Charles Chaney asks his mother to describe his older brother to him, she responds, "I done told you a hundred times—you his spitting image. He was tall and lanky just like you is. He had such a soft face and the sweetest disposition. Just like the Holy Bible say, Junior was black but he was comely" (139). At this point, Jesse Chaney, pushing an alternate aesthetic, intervenes, "He was black *and* comely," he corrected, proudly. "Ain't no *buts* about it" (139–40).[17]

Like Hurston and Wright before him, Killens makes ample use of folk political humor. In *'Sippi*, he gets mileage out of an old joke about the Civil War. Two young fellows engage Deacon Jimson in a ritualistic joke:

> One of them asked him, "Grampa, will you settle a argument for us? Who won the Silver War? The North or the South?"
>
> Rafe Jimson didn't have to study a second about it. "White folks won it," he told them without blinking, as if surely they must have known the answer to such an obvious question. His tobacco-chewing cronies sitting on his porch with him laughed and chuckled their agreement. And spat tobacco into the yard, stream after stream.
>
> The young men roared with laughter. "Grampa, you something else!" And they walked off up the road. They had asked him the same question (must've been a hundred times) and always got the same response. "White folks won the Civil War."
>
> "That's how come you ain't free yet," he shouted after them. "Cause you didn't win it. Git your hindparts down to

that courthouse next Wednesday morning and registrate!"
(262–63)

Killens, of course, does not settle for simply replaying the joke.
In this brief scene, he illustrates a sense of community, positive
interaction among different generations, and political advocacy.

In *Youngblood*, Fat Gus relates a version of a common witticism
about a Black man attempting to subvert segregation: "He went
into this uppidy restaurant in Washington, D. C. and the cracker
waiter walked over to him and asked him was he looking for
somebody—see. The Negro said I ain't looking for nobody, I want
something to eat. Cracker waiter told him we don't serve no
niggers in here. Colored man looked at the waiter and told him—
Man, I don't want no niggers for breakfast. Just give me some stew
beef" (109).[18] As with the "'Sippi" folktale, the author includes
this story as an argument to contest a racist social order.

There are literally hundreds of vernacular examples in *Youngblood* and *'Sippi*, and they contribute greatly to why Killens's fiction was valued highly by proponents, especially the critics, of
the Black Arts Movement. The valorizing of Black folk culture,
the view that art was instrumental or expressly rhetorical, and the
focus on collective political struggle with emphasis on the realiza-
tion of Black manhood all match the prescriptions those critics
would formalize. Killens himself, however, shied away from the
"Spiritual Father" tag hung on him by Addison Gayle.[19] As Gayle
was aware, lines of literary influence can be difficult to draw in
terms of rigid validity; he nevertheless saw Killens as the "leading edge" of a configuration of novelists that includes John A.
Williams, Ernest Gaines, and William Melvin Kelley.[20] Killens
thought more credit should be given to writers from whom he
had himself drawn inspiration. The two most readily apparent
were Du Bois and Wright (despite the latter's markedly different
projections of Black families). He also felt indebted to Langston
Hughes and Margaret Walker, both of whom exhibit in their work
tremendous love for Black people along with visionary, at times
politically radical, outlooks.[21]

chapter 2
Solomon,HighlyLiterate

The reintegration of Solomon "Solly" Saunders, Jr., into the African-American grassroots community is the central movement in John Oliver Killens's 1962 novel *And Then We Heard the Thunder*. Solly grew up in Harlem and as a boy was once chased by the police for aiding fellow African Americans during a riot. However, after proceeding to become college educated and making it two-thirds of the way through law school, he is pursuing bourgeois individualism as opposed to community-oriented activism. He is one of the "exceptional men," a potential savior, even more educated than fellow Du Boisians Richard Myles, Charles Othello Chaney, and David Woodson.[1] He is the most elaborately and vividly drawn, as well as most cerebral, of the host of Du Boisian characters in the Killens canon. As much as any figure in African-American literature, he has felt his "twoness," the competing strivings warring inside one dark body.[2] Ideally, he would like to, as he personifies Du Bois's notion of double consciousness, "do my dancing in the Empire Room at the Waldorf but at the same time keep in touch with my folks who will still be stomping at the Savoy" (5).

After the United States enters World War II, Solly is inducted into the army. At the urging of his new bride, Millie, and propelled partly by his own beliefs, he enters the military determined to strive for personal success within its existing parameters; his plans include being admitted to Officer Candidate School. He is not looking to challenge the segregated system. His view is that in times of war American ethnic groups should unite against a common external enemy and settle their "in-house" differences at a later date. He is reluctant to adopt the motto "Double V," a call for both victory over fascism abroad and victory over white supremacy in the United States, an ethos embraced by many of the more than one million African-American soldiers who served during the war. Although the war was being waged, according to U.S. propaganda, to make the world safe *for* democracy, many African Americans had ample reason to fear for their well-being *in* the so-called democracy in which they lived. Black soldiers were serving both against and with the enemy, and uncompromised Black men like Joseph "Bookworm" Taylor, Jerry Abraham Lincoln "Scotty" Scott, and Jimmy "Quiet Man" Larker choose to resist continually, whatever the cost or personal loss, the adversary with which they are most familiar: the American white man. Solly himself cannot perpetually endure the emasculating abuse and indignities he suffers solely because of the color of his skin, and he eventually adopts an attitude like that of Scotty and the others.

After entrenching Solly in his ethnic peer group, Killens unfolds the remainder of the novel along lines similar to those in *Youngblood*. The major characters are confronted with increasingly harder obstacles that test their unity and resolve. Solly, also known as Sandy, grows stronger in his role as company spokesman. As Scotty announces to white officers during a successful protest against the segregated Post Exchange in California, "I'm not much of a talker, sir. I'm just naturally bashful, me, but we got Corporal Sandy here to speak for me and all the rest of the poor mistreated colored soldiers" (220).

At the beginning of the novel, Solly possesses the talent but not the strength of character to provide committed leadership. Thus the trials and tribulations he experiences serve as preparation. He sheds the illusion that he can be satisfied with individual success that is devoid of dignity and social responsibility or, more specifically, anti-racist combat. By the novel's conclusion, such fighting is perilously real, and Solly proves equal to the challenge as he expertly commands African-American troops during the race riot in Bainbridge. He is not involved in the outbreak of the skirmish; his personal safety is assured. But if he, being the most skilled, intelligent, and articulate tactician among the

African-American soldiers, refuses to participate in the battle, he condemns all the warring Black soldiers to death. Most perish anyway, but many whites die also. As he does in *Youngblood* and *'Sippi*, Killens offsets African-American loss with white casualties. White survivors, faced with the distinct possibility of their own demise, perceive, either rationally or through fear, the absurdity of the battle and cease their participation. Killens thus asserts, once again, the centrality of Black self-defense—along with dedicated high-level Black intellects—to fundamental social transformation.

Gatsinzi Basaninyenzi argues in "Ideology and Four Post-1960 Afro-American Novelists" that *And Then We Heard the Thunder* along with *Youngblood* typify "the integrationist tradition in Black American literature" (7). He contends that after *And Then We Heard the Thunder* Killens rejects such integrationist writing in favor of Black nationalism and its accompanying artistic ideology, the Black Aesthetic. However, Basaninyenzi's critical assessment is questionable, for Killens's early novels reflect several ideologies. There are Marxist leanings and civil integrationist gestures, as well as heavy overtones of Black nationalism. In addition, Killens's aesthetic was overwhelmingly Black from the outset. The linear reading by Basaninyenzi of Killens's novels is therefore too simplistic, largely because he distorts and overemphasizes the author's own analysis in "Reflections from a Black Notebook" that his novels became increasingly Blacker: "From *Youngblood* (1954), my first novel, to *The Cotillion* [1971], it has been a long sometimes tortuous but eventful journey. . . . Each book got Blacker than the one before, I hope. Which means, to me, that each book became more humanistic and universal. It has not been an easy struggle. The journey to Blackness is a rocky road" (12). What the ellipsis conceals is that the author clearly saw himself as operating within a Black Aesthetic paradigm before the term was even in vogue. The missing words: "The people and material of *Youngblood* taught me to tell their story in their words, in their own style, in Afro-Americanese, with Black nuances and Black rhythms and Afro-American idiom. It is what I was consciously into in *Youngblood*

and developed it from book to book until finally, *The Cotillion*"
(12). The deleted sentences and the qualifier, "I hope," which
ends the sentence that follows the recovered statement, are thus
significant.

It is true that Killens's public posture appeared more Black
nationalist by the 1970s. By then he was aware of the Black Arts
Movement—Larry Neal is mentioned in *'Sippi*—and enjoyed an
expanded, nationalist audience, which he cultivated with vigor. It
is also true that he had witnessed the failure of organizing efforts
like that of the CIO and had become disillusioned about cross-
ethnic strategies. But these developments are not *textual* evidence
that his later work is "Blacker" than *Youngblood* and *And Then We
Heard the Thunder*. That issue is still debatable. Surely Robby's
dreams in *Youngblood* are as nationalist as any other statements
made by Killens. Black and white armies fight and the Black army
wins. Armageddon tales in a Black, idiom-filled, folkloric novel.
What could be more "Black Aesthetic"?

Integration in a strictly civil sense has little to do with Killens's vision in *Youngblood* and *And Then We Heard the Thunder*.
Cross-ethnic alliances have to do with gaining and sharing economic and institutional power. They are about justice, not civility
and socializing. So rather than viewing, as does Basaninyenzi,
the donation of blood by Junior Jefferson (it is not Oscar as
he states erroneously) as a crucial symbol of integration, the
act can alternately be read as Killens's radically pluralistic de-
construction of purely racialized motivation. The point for him
is not that the Junior Jeffersons and Joe Youngbloods of the
world should unite just for the sake of interethnic harmony, but,
rather, that phenotype should not ultimately impede collabora-
tion on serious, even life-and-death, issues. In the same vein,
Bob Samuels, at the end of *And Then We Heard the Thunder*, is
not the white liberal Basaninyenzi labels him (though he mis-
takenly calls him Samuel Rutherford). Samuels sides with Solly
and the African-American soldiers during the race riot, actually killing white soldiers to save Solly's life. Solly then terms
Samuels a colored man, a label Samuels rejects, preferring to

affirm that he is a white man capable of siding with African Americans—when justice is the issue—in deed as well as word. This is not liberalism, but action far more radical. White liberals do not pull the trigger against other whites to save African-American lives.

There is no doubt that Solly's primary identification at the end of *And Then We Heard the Thunder* is with the African-American community. Viewing the bodies of Billy "Baby-Face" Banks, Taylor, and Larker, he muses:

> And he knew what he hoped he would never forget again. All his escape hatches from being Negro were more illusion than reality and did not give him dignity. All of his individual solutions and his personal assets. Looks, Personality, Education, Success, Acceptance, Security, the whole damn shooting match, was one great grand illusion, without dignity. . . . He was a Negro and only with Worm and Jimmy and Baby-Face Banks could he achieve anything of lasting value. And Scotty and General Grant and Lanky. And Fannie Mae and Mama. And Junior. (482–83)

Solly's ultimate act of Black solidarity is to reaffirm his decision to become a writer in order to tell the story of his Black comrades. However, it is also the case, and equally important, that even as he speculates about "a new and different dialogue that was people-oriented" that might come out of Africa and Asia, he describes the small gathering of Black and white soldiers he is now a part of as "the place where the New World is" (485). Solly's expanded and final notion of community envisions African Americans as charter members, with others who can pass some semblance of a "John Brown test" invited into the club. This is neither integrationism nor nationalism, but, as Paul Lehman indicates, utopianism, Killens's strongest and most consistent disposition over the course of his career despite otherwise shifting and subordinate positions (which did not shift as much as various detractors have maintained) on culture, politics, and economics.

Because of the complicated multisubjectivities his characters occupy, and given the authorial multisubjectivity that informs those characters, works like *And Then We Heard the Thunder* do not wear simple tags like "integrationist" well. It is interesting and perhaps ironic in this context to recall that in 1971, Killens, even after the commentary in "Reflections from a Black Notebook," rated his first two novels over *'Sippi*, the novel that signals to some his conversion to Black nationalism:

> Well, you know, like I think two of the great American novels
> are *Youngblood* and *And Then We Heard the Thunder*, but
> then again I may be prejudiced. I thought they were militant,
> ahead of their time, advocated self-defense and struggle, gave
> the literature Black heroes and heroines and were written
> in the Black idiom and rhythms of the people. I mean that's
> what I was trying to do. Consciously. I have a feeling that
> while *'Sippi* was a fairdemiddling novel, relatively speaking,
> it didn't come up to the level of the first two. ("Rappin' with
> Myself" 123)

Paul Lehman, although drawing very worthwhile conclusions overall as suggested previously, also employs too linear a model. A Black psyche in his view represents progression from ignorance, confusion, and self-hatred caused by racism to a stage of enlightenment or, if you will, endarkenment. As he elaborates:

> A black psyche is a process whereby a black individual
> gains a new perspective of himself and his world, based on
> a positive and conscious awareness and knowledge of his
> racial history and culture, and comes to view himself, not
> as a black individual, but as a black individual in common
> with blacks in his community, local and national, and the
> world—a black brother or sister to all blacks the world over.
> (27)

And Then We Heard the Thunder, Lehman further argues, most re-flects this Black psychological development as Solly Saunders matures from lacking a Black psyche to attaining one. The problem here, though not the major one, is that the analysis proceeds from the belief that it is merely a knowledge deficit on Solly's part that stands in the way of group identification. In contrast, however, it is readily apparent that Solly is torn, his Du Boisian dilemma, his Empire Room/Savoy split, his accommodationist/activist schism, precisely because he has an abundance of knowledge, not because he lacks awareness of his heritage. He has always felt a community impulse, thus his actions as a child in the Harlem riot; it just has been layered over with bourgeois aspirations. His subsequent affiliative spirit results not simply from information gained in a detached manner but from insight forged, in cyclical fashion, within the experiential crucible. The end product of this process with respect to fellow Blacks is not merely recognition of commonality but commitment. In other words, Solly eventually hops off the psychic fence and starts making choices that reflect a Black psyche, one that he possessed in some measure all along.

Implied in the linear textual approaches of Basaninyenzi and Lehman is a characterization of Killens's theoretical development as a straightforward unfolding in response to societal developments between, say, 1950 and 1970. Neither seems aware that much of *Youngblood*, *And Then We Heard the Thunder*, and *'Sippi* was composed simultaneously, that is, many sections of all three novels were written *before* the 1954 appearance of *Youngblood*. *And Then We Heard the Thunder*, in fact, is the novel Killens was bursting to write when he reentered civilian life in 1945. Theodore Vincent, author of *Black Power and the Garvey Movement*, whose family knew the Killens family in the early 1950s, claims that Killens was subjected to censorship. Vincent asserts: "His left-wing friends promised to help him find a publisher and to promote his book when published, but they were not enthusiastic about his plan to write about the race riot; the subject seemed to smack of black nationalism. Killens conceded and turned out a polite novel about the civil rights struggle in the South" (256). One can quarrel with the description of *Youngblood* as a polite concession, but the Vincent anecdote, seemingly accurate in the main, confirms that *And Then We Heard the Thunder* was not strictly a post-*Youngblood* endeavor.[3]

Certain textual evidence compels the same conclusion. The first fiction published by Killens is a military story titled "God Bless America," which appeared in *California Quarterly* in 1952, two years before *Youngblood* was published. It is a story embedded, largely intact, in *And Then We Heard the Thunder*. Set during the Korean War, "God Bless America" opens as an African-American soldier, who is about to board a ship in California headed overseas, anxiously looks for his wife in the crowd. After he locates her, he begins to board the ship with his segregated unit. As the African-American soldiers approach the ship, the band switches from playing "God Bless America" to "The Darktown Strutters' Ball." An excerpt from the story reads:

> They were the leading Negro outfit, immediately following the last of the white troops. Even at route step there was a certain uniform cadence in the sound of their feet striking the asphalt road as they moved forward under the midday sun, through a long funnel of people and palm trees and shrubbery. But Joe hadn't spotted Cleo yet, and he was getting sick from worry. Had anything happened? (207)

In the novel, published ten years later, as Solly's company leaves California for the South Pacific during World War II, virtually the same scenario is depicted:

> They were the lead company in the regiment immediately following the last of the white troops. Even at route step there was a certain uniform cadence in the sound of their feet striking the asphalt road as they moved forward under the midday sun, through a long funnel of noisy people and quiet palm trees and gorgeous shrubbery. But Solly hadn't spotted Millie yet and he was getting sick from worry. Something must have happened to her! (247)

The 1952 version concludes:

> Luke grinned at him. "What's the matter, good kid? Mad
> about something? Damn—that's what I hate about you
> colored folks. Take that goddamn chip off your shoulder.
> They just trying to make you people feel at home. Don't you
> recognize the Negro National Anthem when you hear it?"
>
> Joe didn't answer. He felt his anger mounting and he
> wished he could walk right out of the line and to hell with
> everything. But with "The Darktown Strutters' Ball" ringing
> in his ears, he put his head up, threw his shoulders back, and
> kept on marching toward the big white boat. (209)

The episode in *And Then We Heard the Thunder* winds up:

> Worm grinned at him. "What's the matter, good kid? Mad
> about something? Damn—that's what I hate about you
> colored folks. Take the goddamn chip off your shoulder.
> They just trying to make you people feel at home. Don't you
> recognize the Negro National Anthem when you hear it?"
>
> Solly didn't answer. He just felt his anger mounting and
> he wished he could walk right out of the line and to hell
> with everything. Nothing had changed though. He would
> still do what he had to do. He would take care of himself, he
> would get ahead in the Army, he would come home safe and
> sound to Millie. He would hate it and at the same time take
> advantage of it. There was nothing else that he could do. His
> face filled up, his eyes were warm and misty too. With "The
> Darktown Strutters' Ball" ringing in his ears he put up his
> head and threw his shoulders back, and he kept on marching
> toward the big white boat. (250)

There are, to be sure, differences between the two versions. For
example, Solly is by then an adulterer thinking as much about
his girlfriend Fannie Mae as he is about his wife. Cleo is actually
pregnant; Millie is only pretending to be. But the texts remain

basically the same. *And Then We Heard the Thunder*, then, was being written as early as the 1940s, being composed at the same time that Killens was working on *Youngblood*, a manuscript that itself yielded parts of *'Sippi*. While it is possible that Killens's perspective could have shifted radically by the time the novels were published in 1954, 1962, and 1967, respectively, the point, of course, is that the textual and biographical evidence does not suggest that major ideological ruptures occur among his first three novels.

Additional insight about Killens's mindset before the publication of *And Then We Heard the Thunder* is contained in Maya Angelou's *Heart of a Woman*. Killens was the person most responsible for encouraging Angelou to pursue a writing career and convinced her to relocate from California to New York in 1959 to participate in the Harlem Writers Guild. Angelou, who briefly lived in the Killens residence, comments, regarding the Killens family, "Everyone except Jon, whose nickname was Chuck, talked incessantly, and although I enjoyed the exchange, I found the theme inexplicably irritating. They excoriated white men, white women, white children and white history, particularly as it applied to black people" (32). Even if one does not totally accept Angelou's depiction, it seems rather obvious that there was no profound "break" with integration to be achieved with either *And Then We Heard the Thunder* or *'Sippi*.

Angelou's account also captures the political passion and characteristic humor that saturate Killens's prose. Killens employed a popular joke to urge somewhat reluctant members of the guild to exhibit support for Fidel Castro:

> "There's no time like right now. You know about the slave who decided to buy his freedom?" Small smiles began to grow on the black, brown, and yellow faces. Grace chuckled and bit into her cigarette holder.
>
> "Well, this negero was a slave, but his owner allowed him to take jobs off the plantation at night, on weekends and holidays. He worked. Now, mind you, I mean, he would work

on the plantation and then walk fifteen miles to town and
work there, then walk back, get two hours' sleep and get up
at daybreak and work again. He saved every penny. Wouldn't
marry, wouldn't even take advantage of the ladies around
him. Afraid he'd have to spend some of his hard-earned
money. Finally, he saved up a thousand dollars. Lot of money.
He went to his master and asked how much he was worth.
The white man asked why the question. The negero said
he just wanted to know how much slaves cost. The white
man said he usually paid eight hundred to twelve hundred
dollars for a good slave, but in the case of Tom, because he
was getting old and couldn't father any children, if he wanted
to buy himself, the master would let him go for six hundred
dollars.

"Tom thanked the slave owner and went back to his
cabin. He dug up his money and counted it. He fondled and
caressed the coins and put them back in their hiding place.
He returned to the white man and said, 'Boss, freedom is a
little too high right now. I'm going to wait till the price come
down.'" (41–42)

Angelou recalls the impact the joke had on the immediate audience: "We all laughed, but the laughter was acrid with embarrass-
ment. Most of us had been Toms at different times in our lives.
There had been occasions when the price of freedom was more
than I wanted to pay. Around the room faces showed others were
also remembering" (42).

Although the accommodationist-revolutionary transformation
is worked out in *And Then We Heard the Thunder* involving a host
of reliable narrators, it is unconvincing to argue that the author
was negotiating the exact same psychic movement in real time. A
critical mapping from simple integrationism to simple nationalism
ignores too much. Concerning his major novels, Killens is more
profitably understood as a practictioner of what Bernard Bell, in
The Afro-American Novel and Its Tradition, calls "critical realism,"
a method oppositional to capitalism and generative of figurative

models for an envisioned society. This is a point Lehman hints at. Using one strand of critical method, the "outside" technique that Killens uses, the writer, as Bell explains, "derives exemplary character types from the individual and his personal conflicts; and from this base he works toward wider social significance" (247).[4] Like the noble Rob Youngblood before him, Solly Saunders reconciles personal angst and overcomes obstacles posed by racism to posit or symbolize broad solutions to the oppression of African Americans, which is conceived in terms of both race and class. A certain Black nationalism is always a part of Killens's work; the Black folkloric, vernacular-laced tales and the community-oriented activism and armed self-defense portrayed in his prose make that clear. But there is ever present, mingled with nationalist gestures, the undeniable strand of critical realism that speaks to wider transformation.

The ideologies conveyed in *And Then We Heard the Thunder*, therefore, are transmitted largely through Killens's manipulation of "double consciousness" as a description of mental condition and his use of critical realism as an articulation of vision. In addition, as is the case with *Youngblood* and *'Sippi,* the author bases the formal outline of the novel on a brief text and then employs a major African-American commonplace as the primary structural component. In this instance, the brief text is supplied by Harriet Tubman, and the dominant trope is "literacy for freedom."

The function of the song excerpts in *Youngblood* and the essential folktale in *'Sippi* is fulfilled by Tubman's partial account of a Civil War battle she witnessed, an account that serves as epigraph and is the source of the book's title: "And then we saw the lightning, and that was the guns. And then we heard the thunder and that was the big guns. And then we heard the rain falling and that was the drops of blood falling. And when we came to get in the crops, it was dead men that we reaped."[5] Part 1, "The Planting Season," chronicles the events that Solly and his comrades endure in a segregated unit in the Jim Crow South. The comparison of the section to Civil War strife suggests the views that many African Americans occupy neo-slave status and that the South itself is where you find it. In this instance, it is in the U.S. military. The seeds sown in the soil of a racist army will be grown and harvested over the course of the story. Part 2, "Cultivation," details the California stint of Solly and his unit as they are being primed, even as they are confined to the Booker T. Washington Post Exchange, for slaughter in the South Pacific. As penalty for their activism in Georgia, they are given four weeks, one-third the normal time, to get ready for deployment as a special amphibian force. Part 3, "Lightning—Thunder—Rainfall," portrays the action in the South Pacific, where Black U.S. soldiers die at the hands of foreign so-called enemies. Part 4, "The Crop," in which Black U.S. soldiers die at the hands of white U.S. counterparts— another Civil War—reminds us that the scene Tubman witnessed led to only a partial victory over racialized persecution. Thus the Tubmanesque outline of the book, which houses and serves as complement to the voluminous narration, urges readers to be, like Tubman—and Du Bois as well—socially responsible and heroic.

Solly's gradual conversion is facilitated by the practice of literacy, a development that represents one of the strongest structural ties between Killens's fiction and the African-American literary tradition. Black writers invariably explore connections between literacy events and liberation, an understandable and perhaps predictable preoccupation given that these writers, consciously or subconsciously, have largely considered themselves to be fortunate, in light of the odds against them, to be able to testify and bear witness. No Black writer has ever felt more blessed in this regard, or more responsible, than Killens. He had experienced much of the ambivalence that Solly Saunders does with respect to military involvement and middle-class ambitions, having himself been a law student whose studies were interrupted by World War II and having himself served in a segregated military unit. Like his character, he decided to become a writer during the war. Explaining his choice, he writes:

> After seeing all that blood and shit and suffering in the South
> Pacific, I had been turned by the experiences into some kind

of half-assed revolutionary. With the stench of blood and
shit still in my nostrils, I reasoned that a lawyer was not a
revolutionary by the very nature of his position in society. His
job, no matter how radical his inclination, was to fight for
the rights of people under this system, not change the system,
but to seek justice and equality under a system where no real
justice or equality were possible. Right or wrong, this was my
rationalization for not going back and completing my last year
in law school. ("Rappin' with Myself" 98–99)

Solly first thinks of becoming a writer during his hectic early
days at Fort Johnson Henry in Ebbensville, Georgia: "One of
these days he would write it all down, he promised himself" (28).
His barracks buddies vie for his attention and loyalty. Bookworm
Taylor pulls him toward a community of rebels while William
(Buck) Rogers, who exists as a caricature of Solly's bourgeois side
and reads him best at the outset, affirms Solly's selfish ambitions.
During a round of verbal jousting, Bookworm claims that Solly
is a Race man, thus committed to collective Black advancement.
Buck responds, directly to Solly, "You're a Race man from way
back, all right. And you been racing ahead of the field a long time.
And you aim to keep your distance" (48).

Solly next reflects on writing as he composes wistful poems
about Fannie Mae Branton, a young woman he met in the PX:
"Ever since he could remember he'd had this fierce obsession to
write, to put something down on paper, and he had started many
novels many poems ever since he was ten or eleven or twelve years
old" (56). This description is true of Killens as well. But unlike
the mature Killens, Solly isn't yet consumed with writing's social
instrumentality. So although he feels "man, whole, complete, fulfilled" when writing, the satisfaction is temporary and only real
to the extent that Solly can exist in isolation (56). The more
he is socialized into segregated army life and gets in touch with
his common, "Savoy" side, the closer he moves toward wielding
writing as a political weapon. On a ten-mile hike, where he in-
teracts with his fellow soldiers apart from his position as company

clerk, he experiences "a warm and honest feeling of belonging" (66). When Captain Rutherford invites the men to speak about their troubles, Solly is the only one in the company to address racism in the military, drawing parallels between the Nazis and the American version of Herrenvolk. To be sure, he is still ambivalent about championing wholeheartedly the ideal of Double V, but on several occasions, to his credit, he does stomp with his company when they need him. This occurs much to the consternation of Rutherford, who, needing the continued services and cooperation of his superb clerk, keeps dangling the old trinkets in front of him to dissuade him from activism: promotions, Officer Candidate School, individual success.

Under the influence of alcohol one evening, Solly feels "good and big and comradery" (94) and suggests to the other men that they write a letter to the Black newspapers explaining the racism and hypocrisy at Fort Johnson Henry. However, exposing his hand to that degree would certainly jeopardize his advancement in the army, so he retreats from his own words and resists Bookworm's urging that they follow through on the idea to publish written protest, causing Bookworm to remark about the educated, "Anything they talk themselves into they can talk themselves out of without doing nothing" (96). Solly defers unconditional commitment as long as he can while still enjoying the comradeship of others who are paying heavier dues. Not until he is savagely beaten by the police in Ebbensville is he ready to agitate with the pen, even making a firm decision to abandon law studies to become a professional writer. When Bookworm once again, in response to Solly's complaining, issues the challenge to write up or shut up, they spend hours collaborating on letters to newspapers and prominent officials. Where previously he wavered, Solly now writes his way into the center of the African-American military community:

> We are Negro enlisted men but all of our officers are white and mostly Southern and mostly rabid Negro-haters. Our company commander is Southern to the core, and also of a

Nazi mentality. The one thing he *has* to give Hitler credit for is his handling of the Jews. When we Negro soldiers go into town, we suffer all manner of indignities. We are looked upon with obvious contempt by the white people in the picturesque town of Ebbensville, beaten up with impunity by Ebbensville's finest and the Military Police. Our company commander intercedes on our behalf by sending us on a ten-mile hike. . . . We are voices crying out in a wilderness of hostility and UN-democracy, victims of a cruel, sadistic, perverted, and hypocritical hoax. Some of us feel that we do not need to go four or five thousand miles away to do battle with the enemies of Democracy. They are present with us here and now and spitting in our faces . . . riding on our backs and breathing down our necks. God only knows why we haven't taken matters in our own hands, or when we might— (173–74)

Solly's words not only highlight the contradictions of a Jim Crow military and represent an eloquent expression of the Double V rallying cry, they foreshadow the novel's apocalyptic ending, that is, the race war between Black and white troops in Bainbridge, Australia, a spin on an event that actually occurred in Brisbane.[6] More immediately, his words solidify the bond between the company clerk and his men despite the fact that as punishment for the letters they are rushed into combat without proper preparation.

On the ship to the South Pacific, the increasingly bitter Saunders begins to write a novel about the army and continues to ponder his politics. After subsequently being wounded in the Philippines, he is sent to recuperate in Australia. While hospitalized he receives a copy of Richard Wright's *12 Million Black Voices* from Fannie Mae, who still serves, along with Worm, Scotty, and the Quiet Man, as his conscience and functions in opposition to Millie, Rutherford, and Solly's "great white brother," Captain Samuels. After reading the book, Solly reasons, "If I'm proud of me, I don't need to hate Mr. Charlie's people. I don't want to. I don't need to. If I love me, I can also love the whole damn human race" (362).

Considering the impact of Wright's career on his own, Killens reveals profound respect:

> Richard Wright [is an influence] because of the awesome
> unadulterated power of his writing, his word power, his
> righteous anger, his indignation, his great success, his impact
> on the western world. He made me believe that a Black writer
> could make the literate world stand up and take notice. He
> taught me through his writing that you don't have to be a
> timid writer. You can be bold, you can say what you have to
> say without holding anything back. ("Rappin' with Myself"
> 100–101)

Killens goes on to acknowledge that his favorite books by Wright are not the more popular *Native Son* and *Black Boy* but *Uncle Tom's Children* and *12 Million Black Voices*. He thought there was an emphasis on Black beauty, collectivity, and possibility in the latter two books.

What specific phrasing made Killens rhapsodic about Wright's folk history of African Americans? One can easily understand the admiration of Killens for Wright's lyrical beauty, what the narrator in *And Then We Heard the Thunder* termed Wright's "awesome overpowering word images" (362). For example:

> Our southern springs are filled with quiet noises and scenes
> of growth. Apple buds laugh into blossom. Honeysuckles
> creep up the sides of houses. Sunflowers nod in the hot fields.
> From mossy tree to mossy tree—oak, elm, willow, aspen,
> sycamore, dogwood, cedar, walnut, ash, and hickory—bright,
> green leaves jut from a million branches to form an awning
> that tries to shield and shade the earth. Blue and pink kites
> of small boys sail in the windy air. (*12 Million Black Voices*
> 162–63)

Killens would have been drawn as well to words that speak of the restorative power of certain Black religious practices. He may, in fact, have plucked Saunders's first name from a section where Wright describes a Black preacher speaking "of Daniel, of Moses, of Solomon, and of Christ" (189–90). Because his protagonist's name is Solomon Saunders, Jr., the character is both literally and figuratively the "son of Solomon" and evokes the wise and literary king.[7] In addition, because *12 Million Black Voices* contains more than eighty engrossing photographs, mostly of workers, families, and other groups, Killens had a powerful visual reminder of Black strivings. Finally, Killens would have embraced the call for collective resistance to oppression at the end of Wright's book, an ending akin to several of his own, including that of *And Then We Heard the Thunder*. In Wright's words, "We are the new tide. We stand at the crossroads. We watch each new procession. The hot wires carry urgent appeals. Print compels us. Voices are speaking. Men are moving! And we shall be with them" (241).

The identification Solly achieves with the "12 million" and his fellow Blacks in the military is facilitated by the vernacular. As in *Youngblood* and *'Sippi*, African-American folk practices are integral to psychological development. For example, *And Then We Heard the Thunder* literally begins with a blues:

> UNCLE SAM AIN'T NO WOMAN
> BUT HE SURE CAN TAKE YOUR MAN—(3)

The narrative then commences: "That was the very very funny song some guitar-playing joker sang like Ledbelly at Solly's wedding reception just a few days ago when he was a newly wed civilian" (3). This blues opening signals that Solly, like all blues sojourners, is going to be severely tested. As the tribulations unfold, Solly recalls lyrics from additional blues songs and other African-American popular music at particularly stressful junctures. Feeling pressure from his wife and mother to advance in the military and at the same time move cautiously enough to survive to resume legal studies, he recalls words sung by Bessie Smith and Billie Holiday (137). Later on, under the strain of battle, he remembers songs like James Weldon Johnson and Rosamond Johnson's "Lift Every

Voice and Sing" (298–99). Folk lyrics are central to Solly's first real bonding with his fellow Black soldiers. On a company march, he joins in as Black soldiers change the lyrics of "Parlez-vous":

> They say this is a white man's war,
> *Parlez-vous;*
> *They say this is a white man's war,*
> *Parlez-vous;*
> *They say this is a white man's war,*
> *Well what the hell are we fighting for?*
> *Hinky, dinky, parlez-vous-* (67)

African-American song traditions and their improvisational quality are thus essential elements of the book. The story may even be said to have a blues ending as ten soldiers sit on the sidewalk in the aftermath of the race riot. They are at the crossroads, so to speak, looking for direction in a place that Solly asserts "the New World is" (485).[8]

Folktales also serve as models of behavior. One example occurs as the new Black recruits, being introduced to military life, are continually referred to as "boys." In response, Bookworm Taylor asks a captain whether the Blacks were in fact in the army, a question that initiates the following exchange:

> "Of course you're in the Army, boy. . . . Where in the hell did you think you were? The goddamn Boy Scouts?"
>
> Bookworm answered softly and sweetly as if he were licking an ice cream cone, "I *thought* we were in the Army, Captain, sir, with all these soldier suits and everything, all this 'Hunt, Hu, He, Ho,' and all that foolishness, marching up and down all day long, but you keep calling us *boys*, so I thought maybe we were somewhere else, cause I read in the *Daily News* where Mr. Roosevelt, the commander-in-chief his-self, said he wasn't going to bring nothing but men in the Army. Gonna leave the boys alone right long in here. So if I'm a boy, I just wondered if you could arrange it so I could go right back

home to Mama and Papa, please, sir. I sure do miss em and
I'm a heap too young to die on foreign soil. Khaki don't
become me nohow. You understand—" (19–20)

For his oration, Bookworm is removed to the guardhouse. His
desire to be released from duty is sincere, but he is also announcing
that if he is to serve, he will do so while insisting on his dignity and
manhood. Bookworm's words represent a spin on a series of tales
and sayings that convey the central message of "call me Mister."[9]
A one-line example, which appears in the *Encyclopedia of Black
Folklore and Humor* under the title "To Whom It May Concern,"
simply states, "Don't call a Black man 'boy' unless he's under ten
years of age" (454). The advice and Bookworm's rendition of it
highlight Solly's dilemma at the outset of the novel. In other
words, he has to decide which compromises of identity are worth
making to achieve mainstream success.

Call-and-response, one of the Black modes of discourse, is another vernacular feature included in the novel, most notably the
interplay among Solly, Scotty, and Bookworm. Scotty habitually
gets into trouble with the establishment, difficulty in which he
typically embroils Solly. Finally, Solly asks, "Why do you fuck
with me so much, man? There are millions of other people in this
Army" (221). Scotty replies that he likes Solly the best and will be
supervising his activity. He states his intentions toward Solly em-
phatically: "Make a man out you or break you" (222). Killens symbolizes the relationship between Solly and Bookworm, and by extension with the other Black soldiers, by using call-and-response
formally. During a discussion of written material supplied by the
War Department, we witness the ensuing actions and words:

But even Worm agreed and shook his big face up and down
when Solly argued that there was nothing wrong with the
War Department propaganda. The thing was, it was never put
into practice.
    "This is good stuff. This is how our country has never
been, but this is how we want it to be. If we can use their

propaganda to make things better for us—now—and after the war is over, what's wrong with that."

Worm shouted from the Amen Corner: "Ain't nothing wrong with that."

Solly said, "We can say, 'Here it is in black and white—in your own words. Now let us practice what we preach!'"

Worm said, "Ain't nothing wrong with that." (270)[10]

Through call-and-response, as with the blues and folktales, Killens further illumines Solly's tie to Black struggle. Solly proceeds haltingly at first, but he ultimately gains confidence in his commitment. He emerges as Killens's most fully developed and expertly drawn protagonist.

chapter 3

Patriots_{and}Radicals

As the career of John Oliver Killens as a fiction writer unfolded, he also wrote nonfiction cultural and political commentary. The 1965 collection of essays titled *Black Man's Burden* stands as his major statement in the genre. But another popular treatise, one not generally associated with his name but to which he contributed, is "Statement of Basic Aims and Objectives of the Organization of Afro-American Unity," a document made public by Malcolm X on June 28, 1964.

The OAAU was the organization that Malcolm founded, or was attempting to establish, upon his return from Africa, a trip that followed his break from the Nation of Islam in early 1964.[1] The creation of the OAAU, according to George Breitman, signaled the beginning of Malcolm's final or most revolutionary ideological phase. As a spokesman for the Nation of Islam, Malcolm championed racial pride and uplift, but such exhortation remained wedded to a political philosophy of separatism and an organizational policy of abstentionism regarding Black political initiatives by others. After a transition period of several months during which Malcolm began to imagine a better political role for himself, he began the OAAU with the intention of leading a broad-based secular entity that would push an agenda of Black political empowerment.[2] Although an emphasis on Black self-determination would continue to be the core belief expressed by Malcolm, his emergent views, in Breitman's analysis, were also pointedly anticapitalist and more global as he conceptualized the Black struggle in the United States in the context of a worldwide rebellion against oppression. Breitman also notes that Malcolm, although he certainly did not stress the idea, admitted the possibility of

59

solidarity with white allies. This "final phase," then, is allegedly marked by Malcolm's more elaborate and mature statement of his Black nationalism, what Breitman describes as a movement from "pure-and-simple black nationalism" to "black nationalism plus" (68). The "plus," in Breitman's mind, involved an impending embrace of socialism.

Breitman's view is hardly definitive. Michael Eric Dyson argues in *Making Malcolm* that "the nature of Malcolm's thought during his last year was ambiguous and that making definite judgments about his direction is impossible" (70). There is truth in both assessments. The point here, however, is that the Malcolm described by Breitman would have great appeal to Killens.

Malcolm and Killens met on several occasions at various venues, including the Killens residence, to work on the OAAU charter.[3] The author considered Malcolm to be his brother, both emotionally and ideologically, and *Black Man's Burden* and the OAAU charter are certainly "brother" texts.[4] Several essential passages appear in both. For example, it is stated in section 6 of the OAAU document that "we must launch a cultural revolution to unbrainwash an entire people. . . . Culture is an indispensable weapon in the freedom struggle" (563). In "The Black Writer Vis-à-Vis His Country," Killens writes that "a cultural revolution is desperately needed, here and now, to un-brainwash the entire American people, black and white" (*Black Man's Burden* 26). In the OAAU document, "entire people" refers specifically to African Americans. In *Black Man's Burden*, aimed at an expanded audience, European Americans are included in the equation.

The need for a cultural revolution is expressed further in the OAAU charter. Given that "our history and our culture were completely destroyed when we were forcibly brought to America in chains," it is concluded that "now it is important for us to know that our history did not begin with slavery's scars" (563). In "The Black Writer Vis-à-Vis His Country," Killens asks, "Who will write the songs for us to sing of our black heroes? . . . Who will recreate the ancient glory that was Timbuktu and Kush and Ghana and Songhay? It is important for us to know that our history on this earth did not begin with slavery's scars" (45).

Black Man's Burden and the OAAU charter also advance the same policy with respect to the social organization of the Black community. Section 5 of the charter calls for the creation of community-controlled drug rehabilitation centers, facilities for unwed mothers, health clinics, senior citizen homes, and orphanages. Also articulated is the need for a concentrated community effort against organized crime and for the establishment of a guardian system to direct Black youth. "We must take pride in the Afro-American community," it is declared, "for it is home and it is power" (563). In the essay "Downsouth-Upsouth," Killens notes that "we must make the Harlems of the U.S.A. sources of black strength, political and otherwise. For as my son, Chuck, wrote me after exposure to the Negro community of Washington: 'I suddenly realized that the Negro ghetto is not a ghetto. It is home'" (*Black Man's Burden* 94).

Obviously, the OAAU charter was composed while Killens was at work on the six essays to be included in *Black Man's Burden*. Perhaps an interesting question is which influence was greater, that of Malcolm on Killens or that of Killens on Malcolm. According to John Henrik Clarke, who also assisted with the charter, he and Killens made no exceptional contribution, mostly helping Malcolm commit to paper ideas he articulated orally.[5] This may, however, be an understatement. Malcolm indeed had a great impact on Killens, but it stands to reason that the author of *Youngblood* and *And Then We Heard the Thunder* was more than a recorder and that Malcolm profited significantly from their exchange. Textual evidence suggests Killens had a fairly active role in the charter's construction. In addition to the letter written by Killens's son, in the one other instance where the line of influence can be positively determined, Malcolm is quoting Killens. As the conclusion of the OAAU charter reads: "When the battle is won, let history be able to say to each one of us: 'He was a dedicated patriot: *Dignity* was his country, *Manhood* was his government, and *Freedom* was his land' [from *And Then We heard the Thunder*, by John Oliver Killens]" (564).

Inseparably linked, though not identical in import, the OAAU charter and *Black Man's Burden* also share rhetorical strategies for the most part. Both are largely ethical, *ad populum* appeals, nestled in the disparity between the American ideal—expressed in documents like the Declaration of Independence and the Constitution—and the American reality of racialized oppression. As stated in the preamble to the OAAU charter, "The Charter of the United Nations, the Universal Declaration of Human Rights, the Constitution of the U.S.A. and the Bill of Rights are the principles in which we believe and these documents if put into practice represent the essence of mankind's hopes and good intentions" (559). Similarly, "The Black Writer Vis-à-Vis His Country" opens with the following paragraph:

> I believe it was George Bernard Shaw who once said that America was the first country in history to go from barbarism to decadence without going through civilization. I construe the statement of this estimable British gentleman of letters to mean that our country has been in such a hurry becoming the wealthiest and the most powerful nation in the world, it has hardly had time or stomach for the niceties of culture and civilization. Indeed, it has been in such unseemly haste, it has not even taken the time to bring into reality some of the most magnificent literature ever written about the rights of men. I refer, of course, to the Bill of Rights, the Declaration of Independence, and the Constitution of the United States. (25–26)

To the extent that faith is expressed in America's civil covenant, both Malcolm and Killens have evoked the African-American jeremiadic tradition, which itself is a variant of the dominant American one.

According to David Howard-Pitney, the rhetorical structure of the American jeremiad includes a citing of America's special and divine promise, chastisement because of present moral slippage or declension, and prophecy that the nation will transcend its decline and achieve its full potential (8). This construct, traceable to the identity formation of seventeenth-century New England

Puritans, who saw themselves as "chosen," was a staple of con-
demnatory sermons by Puritan ministers and still forms the core of
America's civil religion. African-American appropriation of the
American jeremiad posits Blacks as a chosen people—among a
chosen people—and thus, as Howard-Pitney points out, "characteristically addresses *two* American chosen peoples—black and
white—whose millennial destinies, while distinct, are also inex-
tricably entwined" (15).

The public figures who most consistently epitomized this
African-American jeremiad were Frederick Douglass, W. E. B.
Du Bois, and Martin Luther King, Jr.—all leaders who influenced
or interacted with Killens substantially.[6] Although all three by
the end of their lives, and probably Killens as well, were rather
doubtful that America, as a nation, was capable of renouncing its
practice of racial inequity and oppression, the general optimism
evinced by the three great leaders at the height of their respective careers still appealed to Killens in 1965. Their spirit informs
much of *Black Man's Burden,* including the hopeful conclusion,
where Killens poses the question of the correct development to
pursue following the defeat of racism. Concerning white people,
he wonders, "How are we going to integrate them into our New
World of Humanity where racial prejudice will be obsolete and the
whiteness of their skin will not be held against them, though neither will it afford them any special privileges?" (149–50). Strictly
speaking, the question is moot at this point; it is only germane
when the liberation referred to actually occurs, although it must
be acknowledged that *how* racism is defeated impacts the *how*
of the New World of Humanity, a point King would later stress.
However, as Killens wishes to hasten the process, he delivers his
appeal from the brink, in a sense, arguing that the longstanding gap between the national myth and everyday practice—in
particular the disadvantaged position of African Americans in a
land whose wealth was in large measure created from slave labor
and the overall emphasis on profits at the expense of people—
could soon cast the nation beyond any redemption that can be
claimed peacefully. Never strictly the prophet of doom, however,

he provides his characteristic finale, an ideological collage reminiscent of his novels:

> Come all you who labor for your bread, you radicals and
> liberals and intellectuals, you artists who would change the
> world, you educators, who would *really* educate, you preach-
> ers, priests, and rabbis, you Democrats and Republicans, you
> humanists, you winter patriots who love your country. Come
> and go with us. Man has just begun to live. Hurry! We black
> folk cannot wait another moment. The tide is with us. The
> black commander beckons. We must put our boats to sea. Git
> on board, little chillun. Git on board. (176)

Although *Black Man's Burden* is an amplification of OAAU
tenets, it does differ from the shorter work in several important respects. As mentioned above, the essay collection speaks to a larger,
therefore different, audience. Considerable space is devoted to
Killens's utopianism in the multiethnic sense expressed in *Youngblood* and *And Then We Heard the Thunder*. This broader outlook
and the possibility of multiethnic coalitions are not explicit in
the nationalist call of the OAAU charter. Malcolm X, even at his
most ethnically inclusive ideological stage, focused his energies on
getting African Americans to achieve their full potential in the
context of a Pan-African vision. He never embraced the "city on
a hill" mythology, the notion that white Americans had a divine
mission or were the chosen. Malcolm viewed white Americans
as the oppressors of the chosen. So although for argumentation
purposes he would exploit the variance between, say, the Constitution and contemporary reality, his rhetoric, unlike that of Killens, was never one that presumed enlightened whites—the true
or winter patriots, to evoke Thomas Paine—could be a major force
in the true liberation of African Americans.[7]

Despite this long-term visionary difference, there was ample
immediate common ground, as already indicated, upon which
to stand. The right of Black self-defense, an idea synonymous
with Malcolm X in the minds of many, is also a central premise

of Killens's novels. To be expected at this point, the stances on self-defense reflected by the OAAU declaration and *Black Man's Burden*, even some of the wording, are nearly the same. For example, the OAAU charter suggests that "since self-preservation is the first law of nature, we assert the Afro-American's right of self-defense. . . . Tactics based solely on morality can only succeed when you are dealing with basically moral people or a moral system" (559–60). In "The Myth of Non-Violence versus the Right of Self-Defense," Killens first acknowledges the worth of nonviolence as an organizing strategy. He credits practitioners like Martin Luther King, Jr., whom he greatly admired and considered a friend, with using it skillfully to attract worldwide attention to the plight of African Americans and garner the support of white liberals. However, Killens distinguishes between tactic and philosophy and ultimately insists, parting ways with King intellectually, on the right of self-defense, which, he says, "is the essence of the law of self-preservation, which is the first law of nature" (*Black Man's Burden* 109). He then explains that the major shortcoming of embracing nonviolence wholeheartedly is that "when non-violence evolves, as it has in this case, from a tactic into an ideology, and indeed into a way of life, it presupposes that one's opponent is a moral human being. But there is no evidence to support such a presumption" (112).

This is not the first time Killens criticizes King's brand of nonviolence. In 1963, at the funeral service of three of the girls murdered in the infamous church bombing in Birmingham, Killens, according to Coretta Scott King, made a statement to the audience, before Martin Luther King, Jr., delivered the eulogy, that the tragedy signaled the end of nonviolence as a strategy in the Black Freedom Movement and that African Americans must protect themselves with guns (226). Naturally King disagreed, but neither King nor Killens could ever budge one another on this issue.[8]

Throughout *Black Man's Burden*, Killens rejects the popular notion of integration as well, arguing that "integration with dignity for the integrated can only come after the fact of freedom" (79).

This is a line of reasoning, when it was repeated in a 1966 *Negro Digest* article, that drew a negative response from King, who engages Killens at length in *Where Do We Go from Here: Chaos or Community?*:

> At first glance this [Killens's argument] sounds very good.
> But after reflection one has to face some inescapable facts
> about the Negro and American life. This is a multiracial
> nation where all groups are dependent on each other, whether
> they want to recognize it or not. In this vast interdependent
> nation no group can retreat to an island entire of itself. The
> phenomena of integration and liberation cannot be as neatly
> divided as Killens would have it.
>   There is no theoretical or sociological divorce between
> liberation and integration. In our kind of society liberation
> cannot come without integration and integration cannot
> come without liberation. I speak here of integration in both
> the ethical and political senses. On the one hand, integration
> is true intergroup, interpersonal living. On the other hand, it
> is the mutual sharing of power. I cannot see how the Negro
> will be totally liberated from the crushing weight of poor
> education, squalid housing and economic strangulation until
> he is integrated, with power, into every level of American life.
> (61–62)

King acknowledges that Killens's perspective might be valid if the Black struggle for freedom were against colonialists who would be expelled from the country. Given, however, the fact that the United States was home to both the oppressed and the oppressor in the matter under discussion, King ultimately reiterates his belief that "liberation must come through integration" (62). Like the impasse about nonviolence, Killens and King would not resolve this disagreement. More often than not, Killens remained fairly close to OAAU doctrine and more in line with the thinking of Malcolm X. He could, however, have lived comfortably in King's ideal world, and King in his.

Black Man's Burden, besides positioning Killens somewhere between Malcolm X and King, also addresses several of his long-standing concerns, each touched on in his novels: positive Black images, the need to tell an accurate history of enslavement, the importance of teaching African-American history and culture in schools. He rails, for example, in "The Black Psyche," against media proliferation of Uncle Tom or Gunga Din stereotypes, which, in his view, impede any real understanding of African Americans by others. The Gunga Din metaphor, spawned by Rudyard Kipling's "dirty 'ide—white inside" creation, becomes, in fact, central to the psyche of Mr. Wakefield in '*Sippi* and governs his relationship with Charles Othello Chaney, whom he counts on to become a Gunga Din and side with the exploiters against his own people.[9] As part of his criticism of the media, and of movies like *Gone with the Wind*, *Virginia*, and *Kentucky*, Killens insists that images of African Americans be more richly rendered. He says that contrary to the idyllic depiction of slavery in these movies, his own research showed that slaves had been ever subversive and insurrectionist, often burning the very cotton patches they labored in. This insight would directly inform the climactic scene of his 1969 novel, *Slaves*, in which the enslaved workers burn the cotton patch as Jericho and Cassy escape.

In "The Black Writer Vis-à-Vis His Country," Killens deplores the fact that an African-American child rarely saw a reflection of himself or herself either in the popular media or in schoolbooks, a potentially debilitating blow to a Black child's self-esteem. In prose that would fit unobtrusively into current tracts about inclusive curricula, Killens argues that children need to develop positive cultural identities by being taught that their ancestors made valuable contributions to world civilization. He recalls the positive impact made on his son, Chuck, by Langston Hughes, who, on a visit to the Killens home, gave him a copy of *Famous American Negroes*, which Hughes himself had written. Like the French needed a legendary figure like Joan of Arc, Killens subsequently reasons, African Americans need to be taught about Saint

Harriet of the Eastern Shore, referring to Harriet Tubman, one of his sources of inspiration.

Subsequent to *Black Man's Burden*, which ultimately has to be viewed as no less than a sparkling African-American jeremiad, Killens continued to publish regularly about culture and politics. In a 1966 essay titled "Broadway in Black and White," he points to the impressive accomplishments on stage, screen, and television by the likes of Lorraine Hansberry, Harry Belafonte, Sidney Poitier, Bill Cosby, and Cicely Tyson. However, he believed that African-American cultural contributions would have been much greater if not for the racism of the entertainment industry. Accordingly, in his view, African Americans must, simultaneous with pushing for further achievement inside the establishment, create their own cultural institutions. This type of thinking led to the formation, in 1969, of the Black Academy of Arts and Letters, presided over by C. Eric Lincoln, with Killens serving as vice president. A companion article, "Hollywood in Black and White," disparages Hollywood's constant production of negative stereotypes, particularly those of Native Americans and, of course, African Americans. Killens claims that "the Negro is the nation's mid-century protagonist" and must be central to any fresh and dynamic tale about America, a positioning that, to him, can only be rendered authentically by African-American writers (405).

Because of his deep concern with Black heroes, Killens was predictably outraged along with many African Americans by William Styron's 1967 novel, *The Confessions of Nat Turner*, a number one best-seller that was awarded the Pulitzer Prize. John Henrik Clarke solicited responses from ten writers, of whom Killens was one, for an anthology titled *William Styron's Nat Turner: Ten Black Writers Respond*, which was published in 1968. In "The Confessions of Willie Styron," Killens suggests that the white public loved the book because it confirms myths and prejudices against the Black man and attempts to reduce Turner's stature as a historical figure. Killens complains that "Nat Turner, in the tradition of most black Americans, was a man of tragedy, a giant, but William Styron has depicted him as a child of pathos" (34). In Killens's eyes, Styron should never even have attempted the novel because his own paternalism and racism necessarily blocked him from apprehending Turner's true motivation. Styron's Turner dotes on kindly masters, an oxymoron to Killens, and is motivated more by lust for white women than the fact of slavery itself. To Killens, Styron's book is clearly inferior as a psychological profile of a Black rebel when juxtaposed against *Black Thunder*, Arna Bontemps's excellent historical novel about insurrectionist Gabriel Prosser.

In 1966 Killens wrote two pieces for *Negro Digest*. The first, "Brotherhood of Blackness," responds to both an essay by Thomas Echewa titled "Africans vs. Afro-Americans," which had appeared in an earlier issue, and a subsequent exchange in the journal between Echewa and African-American writer John A. Williams. Adopting a Pan-Africanist stance, like Du Bois and Malcolm X, Killens upbraids both men for engaging in superfluous and divisive discourse. Killens rejects the question, as it were, choosing instead to stress the interdependent nature of the struggles against racist oppression in Africa and the United States and urging, furthermore, as he recalls the warmth he felt during a 1962 trip to Africa, unity between continental Africans and their African-American brethren.

Killens received a subsequent invitation from the editors of *Negro Digest* to participate in a print forum: "The Meaning and Measure of Black Power." Along with eleven other writers and prominent figures, namely Julian Bond, Eugene Walton, Anita Cornwell, Conrad Kent Rivers, Sterling Stuckey, Brooks Johnson, Francis Ward, Nathan Hare, Eloise Greenfield, Ronald Fair, and Dudley Randall, he would address two sets of questions: (1) Is the civil rights movement at the crossroads?—And, if so, what are the practical alternatives to it? (2) What is your own reaction to the term "Black Power," and why do you feel the national press and the white public reacted as they did to the term? His response was that the civil rights movement had reached not a crossroads but a dead end and that an alternate strategy was required. Citing a growing schism between a Black middle class, wayward in its complacency, and the Black masses for whom economic conditions were worsening, he reiterates his belief that a Black nationalist unity is a necessary prelude to the integrationist aims of civil rights advocates. He embraces Black Power, which is essentially a restatement of OAAU doctrine, but couples the term, in another bit of *argumentum ad populum,* with the nation's supposedly cherished beliefs. Addressing the potential for African Americans to elect responsive Black leadership, as an alternative to unresponsive white leadership, he explains, "If Black Power means anything at all, it means 'one man, one vote.' It means an end to taxation without representation" (35). While Killens usually may have been a bit strident for mainstream civil rights supporters (this is indeed the same article to which King objected), they could hardly argue with a proposal to flex Black voting muscle.

Actually, the harshest criticism Killens received during the period was leveled against him by Harold Cruse, who disparages Killens and his entire career in his now classic *The Crisis of the Negro Intellectual.* Cruse depicts Killens as duplicitous, integrationist, and opportunist. He particularly disapproves of the latter *Negro Digest* article in which Killens wrote: "It seems to me there need be no strong schism at this moment between the advocates of black power and the 'black *bourgeoisie.*' If one of the principal tenets of Black Consciousness is economic power, the starting place is with the black middle class. May their tribes increase. Black Power advocates are no present danger to them" (34).

It was hard for Cruse to fathom that most Black Power theorists were much of a threat to anyone because he viewed their theorizing to be too amorphous and abstract to represent a coherent and powerful system of thought. Insofar as Cruse could decipher the rhetoric of Black Power, he viewed it as more reformist than revolutionary. His stated problem with the Killens article is that it represents, in his view, insufficient class analysis and a glib turnabout for one who previously championed the working class. Cruse flatly misrepresents Killens, giving the impression that the phrase "all power to the black bourgeoisie" is a quote from the article. Killens, who essentially called for a coalition across class lines, said no such thing. Cruse further accuses Killens of waffling on the question of nonviolence, which is certainly not evident from an examination of his essays and fiction. Nonetheless, Cruse vitriolically binds Killens, who never headed any formal political group, to the shortcomings of Black Power in general:

> Nothing better demonstrates the reformist ideology behind
> Black Power than the Killens stamp of approval. Never
> the originator of a single new concept, style, or exposition
> whether in literature or politics, Killens has been the neutral-
> izing temporizer, the non-controversial, moderating lid-sitter
> par excellence. He is not averse to changing his position
> when necessary; but he possesses the reform politician's knack
> of catching on belatedly to all advanced demands and slogans,
> once it is certain that the establishment must bend to popular
> appeal. He then becomes the propagandizing expert just as if
> he were *always* of that opinion. (561–62)

To be dismissive is one thing, but to be accurately so is quite another. It is certainly not true that Killens made no innovative literary contribution. Addison Gayle and William Wiggins, Jr., among others, describe his unique achievement. Nor is it the case that Killens was uncontroversial. As indicated previously, King was moved to rebuke Killens in print. And at the same time *The Crisis of the Negro Intellectual* was published, the so-called lid-sitting Killens was in the middle of an embattled stint as writer-in-residence at Fisk University because he chose to honor the memory of Malcolm X during a campus ceremony. That Killens changed his position when necessary was not the worst of traits. Many have applauded Malcolm X, whom Cruse deems an outstanding leader, for his facility at self-reinvention. Repositioning is not the important issue; our main interest should be in whether the ideological shifts are reasonable. Cruse charges that Killens was largely motivated by crass opportunism. But Killens's 1966 writing is a virtual restatement of what he was writing in 1964, some of it in conjunction with Malcolm, a fact Cruse fails to acknowledge. Indeed *Black Man's Burden*, written before "Black Power" was a popular slogan and a book that is a must read for anyone who would evaluate Killens in 1967, is a work Cruse fails to mention. While it is true that Cruse's problem with Killens was not simply about ideas expressed in the mid-1960s but was based on experiences, like the Ellison review, extending back two decades, the point to be made here is that Cruse, who argues the need for a rigorous assessment of creative output, fails to make such assessment in the case of Killens. He virtually ignores Killens's writings, except for a phrase or two with which he wishes to take exception. However, he offers no real appraisal of the longstanding traits or evolving features of Killens's work.

Killens was not, as Cruse avers, bringing up the ideological rear. After slamming the 1966 article, Cruse writes, "One cannot analyze leadership trends unless it is done within the context of the role of the black bourgeoisie. The problem is—the Black Power theorists have not done so" (562). That is exactly what Killens was trying to do by considering Black Power and the Black bourgeoisie together.

Cruse's criticism of Killens smacks of a personal vendetta, one that perhaps had its basis in old disagreements that took place when they moved in overlapping cultural and political circles in Harlem. Cruse is critical of the entire *Freedom* newspaper crowd and sees Killens as a central figure of a group that Cruse claims never reached out sufficiently to the Black masses. Cruse also ridicules *The Urbanite*, a short-lived magazine Killens wrote for, as a middle-class, integrationist vehicle dominated by the old *Freedom* writers like Killens and Cruse's favorite foil, Lorraine Hansberry. He furthermore deems worthless a debate held at Town Hall in June 1964 during which Killens, along with Hansberry, Ossie Davis, Ruby Dee, Amiri Baraka (then known as LeRoi Jones), Paule Marshall, and Louis Lomax unwisely, according to Cruse, attacked the white liberal establishment as represented at the session by television personality David Susskind, *New York Post* editor James Wechsler, and *Fortune* editor Charles Silberman. He remarks of the affair that "they were accusing white liberals of not being radicals when they themselves did not compose a group with a radical Negro philosophy of any kind" (200–201). Also coming under fire is the Killens-led writers' conference that was held in April 1965 at the New School for Social Research as a tribute to the recently deceased Hansberry. Of the conference he writes, "The Killens literary and cultural entourage [was] approaching the end of its fifteen-year-old reign. This conference was painfully frenetic and pitifully rhetorical, attempting to analyze the Negro writer's cultural precariousness in American society, and the fate of the American Negro in American culture, as a people" (500).

It would be too much of a digression to explore Cruse's problem with Killens in greater detail. Nonetheless, it should be evident that much of Cruse's analysis is exaggerated and fragmentary. For example, Killens, unlike Hansberry, was not the major player relative to *Freedom* that Cruse would have us believe he was. Although *Freedom* was published monthly from 1951 to 1955, Killens did little, if any, writing for the newspaper other than the brief review of *Invisible Man*.[10] And in his diatribe against the so-called backward, upscale publication *The Urbanite*, Cruse, being characteristically short on specifics, never discusses the exact contribution Killens made to the magazine. If he had done so, he would have been forced to reveal that Killens wrote exclusively about blues and spirituals, hardly highbrow preoccupations.

In March 1961, Killens began to write a proposed series of monthly articles about music, but the publication lasted only long enough to feature two pieces. The first, "A Good Man Feeling Bad!" was a tribute to W. C. Handy, widely known as the Father of the Blues. Killens praises Handy as a vernacular artist who forged masterful music from the cultural testimony of common, everyday African Americans. Killens also posits that Handy's long productivity resulted perhaps from the fact that Handy was a "race" man who "never wandered away from the roots of his creative life" (24). Of extreme importance to Killens, consonant with his own artistic aims, was to demonstrate the generative potential of mass African-American sensibility. This aim, as well as the connection to his own fiction, is made even clearer in his second and last article for *The Urbanite*, "The Negro as Music Maker: Some

Reflections on the Origins of Jazz." In a virtual reprise of the Jubilee section of *Youngblood,* Killens stresses that the roots of jazz lie in the Negro spirituals and then devotes most of the article to explaining, this time without the service of Robby Youngblood and Reverend Ledbetter, the double meanings, the fundamental resisting nature of such songs as "Go Down, Moses," "Swing Low Sweet Chariot," "Steal Away Jesus," and of course, Joe Youngblood's top pick, "Walk Together Children." Killens admits that he took some flak from his editor because it was thought he "had gone too far afield or too far back into the field (of cotton)" to suit the magazine's image (7). Indeed his essay stood as an anomaly in the section of the magazine that was labeled "Classics and All That Jazz" and included reviews of the Modern Jazz Quartet, Antonio Vivaldi, and Brahms. But Killens never wavered either in his general enthusiasm for African-American folklore or in his campaign to alter any perception that Black slaves had been a contented, servile, totally unrebellious lot. He would use any forum, and he used *The Urbanite* quite ably, to propagate his message.

Concerning the charge that the Black writers lacked a radical philosophy at the Town Hall event, one need only recall that the affair at Town Hall took place a mere one week before the release of the OAAU charter, which suggests that even by Cruse's standards, Killens ought to be credited with possessing "some kind" of radical Negro philosophy.

Cruse would have Killens shoulder the entire blame for the ideological and artistic deficiencies of any group of which Killens was part, yet, as mentioned earlier, Cruse has not demonstrated that he has given the major portion of Killens's own writing a serious read. There is absolutely no discussion of the three books Killens had written by 1967. And what Cruse could not have known is that Killens would engineer, over the course of the next twenty years, even larger and more important conferences than the New School event. His entourage, if that is the proper term, had not even peaked, much less reached the end of its reign.

What Cruse saw in Killens over time—and what he *knows* he saw, though he is unsympathetic toward it—is the sort of double consciousness described by Du Bois (and which Cruse experienced as well). This tension is a major feature of Killens's fiction, most expertly symbolized by the character Solly Saunders. It is also a quality he addresses in both interviews and autobiographical statements. But Killens was never an integrationist of the sort Cruse imagines. He was much more concerned with justice than mixing. Nor did nationalism ever grab full hold of his intellect, the reason he modifies, in his typical utopian way, certain OAAU statements.

Killens never addressed directly in print the comments made by Cruse, though he was certainly cognizant of them.[11] In fact, he appeared, along with John Henrik Clarke, another Cruse target, on panels with Cruse. Clarke, who eventually did respond to Cruse in print, wrote that "his book is full of anger without creative direction and facts without adequate explanation" (368). Clarke later confided in an interview that the panels they appeared on together were productive and that he and Killens preferred to support the best aspects of Cruse's thinking rather than to squabble with him about personal attacks.[12] Killens was less generous in private, referring to Cruse as "the establishment's informer and a literary hatchet man." He added that "his book might have been important. It could have been something of value, but he flubbed it, due to his own self-destructive vindictiveness and subjectivity."[13]

Killens's problem in the 1960s was not insincerity, conceptual sloppiness, or lack of community commitment. He could theorize well enough and his involvement and generosity are well established. The more problematic quest was for rhetorical effectiveness. Not wedded to narrow nationalism or mainstream integrationism, and operating in a popular sphere dominated by ideas associated with Malcolm X and Martin Luther King, Jr., he tried to reach audiences whose interests were varied. Like any good rhetor, he chose the means of persuasion most suitable to a given situation. In this regard he resembled both Malcolm himself, who did not deliver quite the same message in the mosques that he did on college campuses, and the great Frederick Douglass, who habitually surveyed his audience, checking its ethnic composition, before deciding the specific content and tone of his speech. Killens led no movement, betrayed no organizational trust, promised no social deed he did not perform, impeded nobody else's progressive actions, or promoted any cause incompatible with Black liberation. It made little sense to criticize acrimoniously someone of this character who was grappling with important ideas and struggling to participate in the major discourse relative to those ideas.

The best essay by Killens during the 1960s and early 1970s, "Black Labor and the Liberation Movement," appeared in *Black Scholar* in 1970. He announces that:

> Between us club members in the Brotherhood of Blackness, it is no secret that the Black Liberation Movement is running out of steam. The Civil Rights Integrationist organizations are deathly stricken with senility and obsolescence. The Black Power detachments are at the moment powerless. "Race riots" as a form of struggle have become a terrible bore to the sophisticated White Establishment. Indeed in many cases the metropolitan police forces looked forward eagerly to those famous long hot summers as a means of killing off a few of the "natives" and as a proving grounds for testing new anti-riot weapons. (33)

The biggest weakness the author then saw in the movement was its failure to organize the Black labor force, the most numerous and potentially dynamic segment of the Black community. The working class outnumbered both the African-American middle class, which according to Killens had set too much of the Black political agenda, and the lumpen element romanticized by groups like the Black Panthers. "The vanguard is beautiful, dramatic, inspirational and necessary," he writes, "but the army is where it's at" (34). Black labor is seen as the army, the "Great Black Hope" (34). Killens, the former union official, no longer had faith (if he ever really had) that white labor could organize in the interests of African Americans. Commenting on Marxist thinking, for example, he argues that Marx himself undertheorized the influence of racism and the corruption of the white working class in industrialized nations. He calls for the creation of a National Black Labor Congress and closes the essay with "*All Power to Black Labor!*"

Cruse might call this an example of flip-flopping, and might even take some credit for influencing it. But there is nothing in the article not foretold in Killens's union activities or earlier writing. Notwithstanding, he may still have been thinking of Cruse when he offers in his 1971 self-interview, "Rappin' with Myself":

> I think I'm a man who has made a helluva lot of mistakes
> in my time, but I have always been in there pitching. I have
> always worked for Black liberation, but I've changed my mind
> a million times about how we are going to achieve it. For
> two years I was a CIO organizer. I had hopes that we could
> liberate the nation by joining hands with the white working
> class. Big mistake, but I learned from it. The thing is to learn
> from your mistakes. I was not disillusioned when the working
> class joined the KKK and voted for Wallace (I don't mean
> Henry). I wasn't disillusioned because I had no illusions in
> the first place. I just had high hopes. I was optimistic. When
> the labor movement didn't make it and was co-opted by the
> establishment, I said to myself, "Okay, that's that." I didn't
> really believe it anyhow. How could I? Growing up as I did in
> Macon, Georgia. I don't want to make a fetish or a religion
> out of mistake making. But I do insist upon my right to make
> them if they're not too costly to me and my people, and also
> my right to change my mind, to change me. (121–22)

It remains an open question whether Killens *really* had no illusions about cross-ethnic workers' solidarity. But whatever illusions may have existed could not have been simplistic. He was a brooding thinker and of Georgia, Harlem, Brooklyn, the 1930s, the 1960s, universities, World War II, and the labor movement. His essays reveal this range of experiential tension, the same territory explored in his novels, and make up an impressive complement.

chapter 4

CulturalHeroes

In 1968, in the aftermath of the assassination of Martin Luther King, Jr., Killens wrote an essay, partly in tribute to the civil rights martyr, titled "The Black Writer and the Revolution." He urged African-American writers to remain up to the task of political and cultural transformation. "Make the revolution," he exhorted. "You can be rebels **with** a cause. A rebel-with-a-cause **plus** a program equals a revolutionary" (397). He issued his familiar call for a literature of Black legends, myths, and heroes, works that would incorporate historical reconstruction and visionary insight. The collective African-American literary project, in other words, should celebrate African-American people and promote resistance against oppression, and this artistic outpouring should be presented, according to the Killens prescription, in the African-American vernacular:

> Western man has used language, words, as a powerful weapon
> to enslave the rest of mankind, and now we black writers
> must use our language, Afro-Americanese, to redefine
> ourselves. We black folk are a colony on the mainland. I
> have heard colored musicians themselves say, "I don't play
> jazz, spirituals, rhythm and blues and that kind of stuff. I play
> serious music." I'm saying, these brothers have been had. The
> language has enslaved them just as it has enslaved, on one
> level or another, every black brother and sister in this nation.
> One of the black writer's tasks is to decolonize the language.
> "Good hair" and "high yaller" and "a nigger ain't shit" will
> have no place in Afro-Americanese one of these days, and
> soon, if the black writer does his job. (397)

Killens himself was just beginning to generate a new strand of prose to fit the bill. His first three novels were all developed from notes, scenes, and drafts traceable to the beginning of his career in the 1940s. They sprang largely from his early experiences in Southern and segregated environments. The publication of 'Sippi in 1967, when Killens was fifty-one years old, marked the last major mining of that creative vein. In The Cotillion, published in 1971, Killens turns his attention to the Black, urban North of the late 1960s—sometime after the assassination of Malcolm X but before the murder of King—to continue his abiding interest in exploring and trumpeting African-American communal and political possibilities.

The genesis of The Cotillion, as with most Killens stories, was autobiographical. Club women were trying to get his daughter, Barbara, to become involved in a cotillion at the Waldorf-Astoria. Barbara, however, preferred to be immersed in political protest activities. According to her father, "she was into demonstrating, picket lines, sitting down in front of trucks, getting arrested, etc." ("The Half Ain't Never Been Told" 306). Nonetheless, Killens seized on the vehicle presented to turn out a hilarious satire of the Black middle class and disingenuous Black nationalism, a novel many regard as his best.

Harlem resident Yoruba Evelyn Lovejoy, the story's protagonist, has been invited by the Femmes Fatales, a group of bourgeois Black women who supposedly represent the "first Black families of Brooklyn," to participate in the Grand Cotillion to be held at the Waldorf. Yoruba and four other "disadvantaged" Harlem girls are slated to "benefit" from the missionary kindness of Mrs. Patterson and other members of the organization, who all reside in the relatively upscale district of Crowning Heights, a fictionalized version of the Crown Heights neighborhood in which Killens lived. Yoruba, however, is ambivalent about participating in the pageantry. Her budding Black nationalist identity and aesthetic do not easily accommodate the role of Black debutante, essentially seen as mimicry of white middle-class mating rituals and

standards of beauty. The pressure to participate, to which she suc-
cumbs, is applied by her mother, Daphne Braithwaite Lovejoy,
a light-skinned West Indian mulatto who identifies much more
with European culture than that derived from Africa. By contrast,
Matt Lovejoy, who bestowed the name Yoruba on his only child,
is a Georgia-born, coal-black, frustrated nationalist who has no
allegiance to white mythology and symbolism. He has no illusions about the value of a cotillion for Blacks. White folks, he
understands, devised these events so their daughters would have
a chance to meet, mingle with, and perhaps snare the most desir-
able, wealthy bachelors. But he sees no benefit in slavish imitation
that amounts to no more than "just some more white folks' fool-
ishness that don't git Blacks folks nowhere except in debt" (139).

The folly of valorizing alien mores and symbols, without even
understanding them no less, is further dramatized at a tea hosted
by the Jeffersons, one of the more earthy families associated with
the Grand Cotillion. Mrs. Jefferson strikes up a conversation with
Mrs. Robinson, the mother of Charlene, one of the other "disadvantaged" Harlem girls:

"Do you dig Ray Charles?"
　　Charlene's mother answered in a vague and horrifying
mixture of assorted and affected accents: "Oi don't like jazz,
blues, spearchals and that kind of common averday music. Oi
prefer the classics. Oi like Chopping."
　　Mrs. Jefferson said, "I'm hip. Everybody like chopping. You
have to eat to live, but I thought we were discussing music."
　　"Chopping!" Mrs. Robinson repeated softly, desperately,
breaking into a sweat. "He's a great European musician. He
lives in Paris." Could she be wrong about this too? Why was
Mrs. Jefferson staring at her as if she were a total idiot? Mrs.
Brap-bap saved the day, so to speak. "She means Chopin," she
explained to Mrs. Jefferson. Then to Mrs. Robinson she said,
"Honey, you can't even pronounce him, let alone appreciate
him." (121)

Matt ultimately agrees to support Yoruba's involvement in the pageantry because he unequivocally loves and supports *her*, not because he believes in the activity sponsored by the Femmes Fatales, whom he sarcastically calls the "Fat Asses." His demeanor differs from his wife's, which, though also loving, rests on browbeating and emotional blackmail. She wants to make her daughter as "European" as she can.

Yoruba's very body signifies the ideological struggle between her parents. Her father never fails to appreciate her natural African-derived beauty, as does the author; she is repeatedly described as "Black and princessly." Yoruba's mother, on the other hand, has always sought to refigure her. She used to make her daughter hold her lips in, hoping that would make them grow thin. She also would keep Yoruba out of the sun as much as possible and, following an old superstition familiar to many African Americans, would never allow her to drink coffee. Both actions were taken, of course, to prevent Yoruba from becoming any darker in complexion. Daphne does not hold Matt's color against him. She married him because she figured that he respected and adored her in a way that no white man she had ever met did. But because she felt she had disadvantaged her daughter color-wise, she desired to keep the damage to a minimum and not ruin her chances to mix among light-skinned "cultured" Blacks, marry one, and have light-skinned children with straight hair.

Ben Ali Lumumba, Yoruba's boyfriend and the story's narrator, plays a crucial role assisting her to prepare for the Grand Cotillion while she, in turn, helps him clarify cultural and political conceptions and resolve some of his own self-doubts about Black identity and activism—his own shaky reliance on symbols, for example, including the phony British accent with which he sometimes speaks. Lumumba is also the key agent in the eventual psychological liberation of Daphne. Originally too dark and woolly headed for Yoruba's mother, who is appalled that Yoruba dates him and has chosen him as her escort, Lumumba gradually succeeds in altering her perspective. Her resistance is first diminished when she discovers that the *New York Times* had featured an article about him, portraying him as an up-and-coming writer. Although quick to discount the capabilities of a "darkie," Daphne decides he must have worth if important white folks deem it so. After meeting with Lumumba, who removes his beard, trims his hair, and dons a suit to impress her, Daphne admits to his charm, though she could envision no serious romantic relationship between Lumumba and Yoruba.

Daphne's outlook changes even more when she works as a servant at a white cotillion held in Southhampton. Yoruba and Lumumba also take jobs at the affair, Yoruba because of her mother's pressuring and Lumumba because he has decided to write a satirical novel titled *The Cotillion*. Lumumba wants to work the rich white folks' cotillion, the source of the imitative Black ones, both to gather material for his book and to show Daphne what impoverished and silly events all cotillions are. He explains to Daphne— and Killens explains to us—that he would only attack the African-American bourgeoisie in the context of scrutinizing the actions of the European American bourgeoisie.

For Lumumba's purposes, the trip to Long Island could not have worked out better. In a scene reminiscent of the party at the Wakefield residence in *'Sippi*, the debutante ball degenerates, after parents and press depart, into a raucous orgy. Spurred on by alcohol and marijuana, the partygoers fornicate, or attempt to, all over the estate, engage in drunken brawls, and set the mansion on fire. The police and fire departments are summoned and the "riot" is later reported in the *New York Times*. Throughout the spectacle, Lumumba directs Daphne's gaze to various scenes, working to shatter her belief that the white bourgeoisie possess superior culture and refinement. "Look! Look, Miss Daphne! So this is the great white upper class, the cream of the crop! Wow!" (213). In the face of such stark evidence, Daphne capitulates. Although her psychic movement toward full acceptance of Black culture remains tentative, she nevertheless finds the display of white culture repulsive. She hurriedly leaves the Long Island cotillion, preferring to walk to the train station rather than wait around for the limousine and the return ride to New York City.

While the party only costs Daphne some of her illusions, it cost Killens a measure of commercial success. Motown optioned *The Cotillion* and planned to develop it into a Broadway musical. Smokey Robinson and Willie Hutch were slated to write the music. However, negotiations broke off over the Long Island scene. According to Killens, Bob Cohen, who was in charge of Artistic Productions, was troubled by the depiction of the white characters. The option was allowed to lapse as Killens stood his artistic ground.[1]

Daphne is nearly as stubborn. Not willing to abandon all her dreams for Yoruba, she rationalizes that the Femmes Fatales, unlike the folks in Southhampton, can imbue a cotillion with respect and dignity. She still views the imitation of whiteness to be a legitimate objective. To the contrary, Yoruba and Lumumba decide to subvert the Grand Cotillion, to make it truly Black and beautiful by using it as a platform to critique the festivities. They don African garb; Yoruba wears her hair natural for the first time. After they reach the stage, in a ballroom designed, in line with that year's theme, as a plantation, Lumumba seizes the microphone and, during an uproarious conclusion, exclaims, "Be done with false illusions! Come with us to the real world! . . . Up the Black Nation" (255). Ironically, the Grand Cotillion does serve as the "coming out" for Yoruba—and for Daphne, who joins them, and perhaps Lumumba as well. It was, as Fred Hord points out in *Reconstructing Memory*, "the culmination of their demystification of colonial cultural repression and their resistance to its dehumanization" (100). Priscilla Patterson, who boasts of having the whitest blood in the Femmes Fatales, tries to persuade Daphne to remain with them in their cause. She shouts at her, "You understand!" Daphne responds by standing tall, "taller than she'd ever stood," and declaring, "I understand. Finally I understand. And that's exactly why I going with my people" (255). It is an ending that prompted Charles Johnson to remark, in *Being & Race*, that *The Cotillion* is a " 'positive' Cultural Nationalist comedy shaped entirely by radical black views on art" (91).[2]

Although *The Cotillion* is probably discussed most often because of the degree to which the Black bourgeoisie is ridiculed, Killens criticized members of the Black privileged class in fiction as far back as *Youngblood*. A more significant development is how those "radical black views on art" are structured. The main rhetorical strategies of the novel involve the "Du Boisian veil," the elaborate use of signifying, the recurring figure of Malcolm X, and the revision of community texts both sacred and secular.

As Daphne begins to recognize the silliness of the Long Island affair, her reactions are so described: "Now, at this, the 'really real thing,' the epitome of WASPY culture, a misty veil was slowly lifting from her eyes, even as she struggled valiantly to remain behind the veil of her darling innocence" (213). Du Bois often uses the metaphor of the veil in *The Souls of Black Folk* to represent the effects of racism.[3] The veil does not totally block African Americans' view of the larger society, but it affords a dim and distorted perspective that Blacks must continually labor to transcend. As Stephen Carey points out, an aspect of the "darkened view" is that it produces feelings of cultural inferiority in Blacks (66). Du Bois himself wrote with guarded optimism that "if somewhere in this whirl and chaos of things there dwells Eternal Good, pitiful yet masterful, the Anon in His good time in America shall rend the veil and the prisoned shall go free" (*The Souls of Black Folk* 215). Fortunately, this is the journey Daphne gets to take in the novel, the Anon in this case being the novelist.

Black satire, not merely an adornment, also holds the basic story together. As Lumumba, the narrator of *The Cotillion*, frames the matter in the foreword, "I meant to do myself some signifying. I meant to let it all hang out" (6). Just as examples of Daphne's alienation build toward the lifting of the veil, a series of clever barbs throughout the novel inexorably leads to the conclusion, which is, in essence, one big put-down of a cultural ritual deemed backward by the author. Also targeted for signifying, as a major strand of the book, are so-called Black Powerists who evidence more lip service than long-term productive engagement. They are unable to achieve positive communal construction of any sort, much less the "nation-building" about which they speak so freely. The Killens humor, always a central quality of his prose, is keenly sharpened to attack negative or compromising behavior manifested within or on the fringes of the Freedom Movement.

In the opening pages, Killens symbolizes the disarray of African-American political activity. The Black and Beautiful Burlesque, a strip joint featuring Afro-wearing Black beauties, has become the focus of "pickets picketing pickets picketing pickets, who were picketing" (15). Nationalists were demonstrating against the idea of Black nudity, while integrationists pushed for integrated burlesque queens. The burlesque club, we are told, "was where the action was, and there were fist fights every other night" (15).

Immediately afterward, we meet Billy "Bad Mouth" Williams, "mayor of Black nationalist Harlem," pontificating on the corner of 125th Street and Seventh Avenue. Billy is presented as totally self-absorbed: "God and/or Allah's most precious gift to the lucky Harlem masses. Don't take anybody else's word for it. Check it out with Bad Mouth himself. He'd tell you he was the last of the great Black Nationalists. Uncrowned prime minister of the Black government in exile. Hey! There was Garvey, Malcolm, Bad Mouth Williams. After that—well, Armageddon" (16). Bad Mouth has a variety of stock speeches to appeal to the Harlem masses. He knows the tropes, so to speak. Yoruba does also, for after only a few minutes of Bad Mouth's diatribe against hustling preachers, she muses, "It's preachers today. Yesterday it was 'Negro' leaders. The day before it was the 'white Communist liberals.' Tomorrow he would be doing a putdown on something else. The labor movement. The NAACP. The President." Bad Mouth's talk is not entirely unworthy. The author's own perspective is evident in the accusation that "You don't want no power. You just want to intergrate" (20). But Bad Mouth *only* talks; there is no sign that he is committed to organized and protracted struggle.

Lumumba is cast similarly early in the novel. As the "author," he can be said to be satirizing himself. Discussing with Yoruba his plans to become a writer, he dismisses the poetry he had just performed before a crowd at the Café Uptown Society. "Oh I don't mean that jive I just read. That's for the birds, the Black ones I mean. All you got to do for this crowd here is call whitey a bunch of mother-humpers and say that Black is beautiful, and like you got it made" (68). Later, in a restaurant, a series of Black men approach Lumumba, each offering a creative but overly complicated handshake. Lumumba says to one, "Brother, we got to get ourselves a quicker handshake. Whitey be kicking our heads in while we going through the ritual" (92). Definitely more style than substance are teenage members of the BBBMF, the Black and Beautiful Bad Mother Fuckahs. They cannot even recognize Lumumba without his beard, but once they hear him speak and are certain it is he, they assure him, "You're our main man" (172). They give Lumumba a business card, promise to T.C.B. if he ever needs them, and strut off in their dashikis and alligator boots.

The most memorable political caricature in the novel is that of Jomo Mamadou Zero the Third. Years before Paddy Chayefsky's *Network*, a film in which Black radicals are solicited for a television series in order to boost ratings, the self-styled revolutionary makes an appearance on *The Johnny Carson Show*.[4] Lumumba, a former seaman, shipped out with Jomo off and on for more than a year. That is why he knows that Jomo was not, as he claims, in prison during that time for dealing drugs and pimping. Lumumba anxiously awaits Jomo's appearance, though, because he feels his rap is "good therapy for the souls of Black folks" (173). But if Mr. Zero cannot fool Lumumba, he certainly isn't tricking or co-opting NBC either. To them, he's simply an exotic entertainment pawn. As Carson introduces him:

And now ladies and gentlemen, it is my proud pleasure to introduce to you that greatest revolutionary of all times. He's greater and more dangerous than the late lamented Malcolm X, may he rest in peace and nonviolence, heh heh heh, and with all due respect. When he was two years old, our distinguished guest witnessed his father beat his mother to death with a large hambone. He swore off swine from that day forward. He was raised up by himself in the very jungle wilds of Harlem, hustled heroin and prostitutes since he was eight years old, raped his grandmother at the age of nine. Did five years in Sing Sing. And now he's making plans to overthrow our beloved country and systematically murder all us white folks. Isn't that wonderful? Isn't it truly tremendous? Give him a big hand, fellow Americans. He's gonna kill every white man in this nation. Bring him on with grand applause. Make this great one feel at home. (175)

When Jomo makes his entrance, to wild cheers and applause, Carson greets him, "Jomo Mamadou Zero the Third, ladies and gentlemen. Jomo Mamadou the Third! Sit down right here, Jomo, my main man, and tell us how you're going to overthrow the government and kill all the white folks in the world" (175). Jomo fulfills his part of the bargain as Lumumba watches in silence:

> His main man, Jomo Mamadou Zero the Third, in his boss dashiki, with large black glasses covering the upper regions of his face, glared out from behind his bad black beard at the ocean of pink-white faces in the TV audience. He spat across the footlights at them. And they applauded. He growled, "I wished all of you pale-faced pigs a bad damn evening, you swinish cannibalistic motherfuckas! And after them few kind words of salutation, I'm going to say some mean things to you." And the place exploded with applause. Pale-faced Johnny Carson shouted, "Isn't he wonderful, ladies and gentlemen!" (175–76)

While Killens criticizes some of the affectations and commercialism of 1960s-style Black nationalism and emphasizes that Blacks themselves are sometimes the enemies of Black progress, he yet is dedicated to the idea, as he is in his previous novels, that African-American self-love and unity are the first principles of a true Black liberation movement. Yoruba, for instance, would remind herself that the "hustlers, thugs, hoodlums, and pimps" who memorized

catchphrases, bought dashikis, and changed their names were not
the essence of the Freedom Movement (69–70).

The core of the movement, in Killens's view, are the vast number of everyday hardworking African Americans who would be re-
ceptive to responsive and responsible leadership. The role model
in this regard, the standard by which all leaders are to be measured,
is Malcolm X. At least a dozen times in the story his name is used,
his nobility and dignity evoked, to point out the limitations of
some would-be leader or to affirm a positive action or decision.
Although Malcolm himself did not get to articulate fully his political program, his intellect intrigued Killens and he celebrates
this attribute, along with Malcolm's love and commitment. *The
Cotillion*, as Norman Harris observes, "asserts that symbolic political activity not directed by goals derived from an articulative
philosophical framework is often futile and sometimes cruelly humorous" (154). Malcolm's promise, the potential of coherent and
sustaining direction, the framework Harris speaks of, undergirds
the novel. Killens thus aims to preserve the most generative aspect of Black nationalism, that is, the ethnic cohesion that can
ultimately lead to fundamental social change. He realizes that the
universal, whether in politics or art, is only approachable by way of
a nationalist trail. Or as Hord phrases it, "Killens' correct politics
calls for a hold on transcending nationalism until the prospects
for universalism are black brighter" (87).

The intellectual heart of the novel is Matt Lovejoy. Georgia-
born and in his fifties, like the author in both respects, he is the
most grounded character in the text, and he is the one with a
consistently secure and positive view of himself. Like his biblical
namesake, who provided the first gospel of the New Testament,
Matt preaches his own "first gospel," an amalgam of the Scriptures,
still the most powerful text in the Black community, and Black nationalist myth. His "preaching" sustains his family and influences
the broader community. For example, when conversation in the
Jenkins Palace Barbershop gets around, as one can easily imagine
it often does, to the ethnicity of Jesus Christ, Matt assumes the
"pulpit":

"Let me run it down for you. Fact of the business, Jesus'
mother, Mary, was white. Right? But old Joseph was Black.
Yes he was. That's how come they couldn't find no place to
stop at in any of them Bethlehem hotels. That's how come
there wasn't no place in the inn, cause them peckerwoods
couldn't stand to see old Black Joe miscegenating all day and
all night with little Miss Mary Anne."

Suddenly, it got so quiet you could have heard a bedbug
making water on a snowbank in Siberia. They never knew
whether to take old Matt Lovejoy seriously or not. He was
always coming out of a weird bag nobody else had ever heard
of. Matt continued running down his thing.

"All them Jews were colored in them days. And the white
man, talking about the Romans, they had colonialized
them, and Jesus was a Black Power man and he was trying
to freedomize them. That's how come they crucified him.
A lot of them Jews were toms, and they panicked after Jesus
split, and they went off to Europe for two thousand years and
miscegenated with them white Europeans and passed on into
the white race. That's how come some of them suckers still
got kinky hair, I mean till this very day. They ain't nothing
but light-complected Negroes passing." (32–33)

Killens also links the Bible to popular community discussions
of the question of nonviolence and to his own disagreement with
King. After a character voices support for civil disobedience, one
of the barbers respectfully, though disapprovingly, responds: "I'm
with Rev. Luther all the way. He a good man. God-fearing and
all that jive. But I just can't see myself letting a paddy beat on
me, and I'm just standing around telling the sucker how much I
love him. Telling him to be my guest. I believe in an eye for an
eye and a tooth for a tooth. That's in the Good Book too. And
a head for a head, and some ass for some ass. That's America to
me. That's the true Christianity" (40). Even though Killens began
work on this comedic novel to work out of a depression following
King's bitterly ironic assassination, he would never embrace the

nonviolent aspect of his friend's philosophy. He never believed King got it right and gives Matt Lovejoy the final, homespun word on King's approach: "I know one thing. It stands to reason, if the rabbits took rock-throwing lessons, there wouldn't be all them many hunters pitching boogie in the forest" (41).

As is evident, the political vision and primary topoi are cast in the Black vernacular. Although Killens had admirably employed such discourse as a significant feature in his prior novels, particularly with respect to dialogue and folklore, such discursive practice was framed by or entwined with naturalism or social realism and was never the dominant stylistic feature of those texts. He had written what Gayl Jones terms "composite novels" (13). With the 1970 publication of the short story "Rough Diamond," he freed his voice, as Jones might say (178), and devoted his complete literary canvas to showing off urban Black orality. Of course, this advent squares with the ideas espoused in "The Black Writer and the Revolution," but Killens was able to pull off the maneuver because by then, having lived in Harlem and Brooklyn for more than two decades, his ear had become finely attuned to the Black urban rhythms that surrounded him. "Rough Diamond," especially given its satirical bent, is a warm-up act for *The Cotillion*.

The story lampoons the Black writer-as-charlatan and centers on Bill Yardbird, who wins the National Book Award in 1964 for a book on Harlem in which he mostly traded in social pathology and "showed that jungle in all its true savagery and degradation" (171). Reminiscent of his 1952 review of *Invisible Man*, though ironically Yardbird is his Rinehart, Killens has the narrator exclaim, "I went Ellison one better, baby, ten times better. The father of the hero of my book had knocked up his wife, his mother, his three daughters, all in the same damn month" (171). The Black press denounces Yardbird for being an Uncle Tom or Gunga Din instead of an authentic "diamond in the rough," and he is chased from the community. He lives in Greenwich Village while also maintaining a Harlem address. Yardbird, the ever backward psuedo-militant, eventually ends up behind the Iron Curtain and in bed with Elsatanya, his Russian guide and interpreter. The inspiration for Yardbird is a real writer, whom Killens declines to name, who was on television talking about how he had to get away from the "niggers" in Harlem. The use of the N-word alone, especially when not assigned to a fictional character, was enough to prompt Killens to respond. In current N-word debates, he would surely argue against its general use. He often summed up slavery and colonialism as the niggerizing of the earth and saw no positive place in the lexicon of Afro-Americanese for the word, which he termed the "alpha and omega word of our degradation" ("Rappin' with Myself" 118). To revel in "niggerness," he adds, "is to wallow complacently on the dunghill of our white-imposed degradation like a pig in a pool of mud" (118).

The Cotillion itself reads like a long Black Arts prose poem. The flowing, fast-paced, lean, sparse, "freed-up" writing is inspired by Amiri Baraka, for starters, as Johnson points out, and by Haki Madhubuti as well. As Yoruba is on the "A" train coming from work, "hot air, baby, by the ton, hot air was blown, stirred together by the whirligig electric fans overhead and shaken up by this St. Vitus-dancing, boogalooing, epileptic 'A' Train. Funky Broadway all the time. Funky! Oooh! Yeah! Dig it! Creating one overwhelming impact which rendered Yoruba's senses numb, and the dear child almost senseless" (10).

When Yoruba, now aboveground, strides toward her home, we get the type of impressionistic tribute to jazz that was commonplace among poets of the Black Arts era: "One Hundred and Twenty-fifth Street was also the street of sounds. Magnificent sounds. Jukeboxes all along the main stem blasting out the classics. Blowing love and hate and sorrow. Black classics. Serious music by serious musicians. Max Roach, Ray Charles, Lou Rawls, Etta Jones, Archie Shepp, John Coltrane, horn-blowing horn-blowers" (14).

At the Uptown, Yoruba's initial perception of Lumumba is similar to the narrator's in Madhubuti's 1969 poem "But He Was Cool." Yoruba thinks "the cat on stage was clean. Not clean like Mister TV Clean, but handsome clean, hip clean, fine clean. Clean clean. Black clean" (64). In Madhubuti's poem, a character is depicted as "cool-cool ultracool was bop-cool/ice box cool" (39).

During a prep session for the Grand Cotillion, several members of the Femmes Fatales discover that Matt Lovejoy is a redcap at Penn Station, Pamela La-Smyhte's father is a janitor, and Charlene Robinson's writes the numbers. They exclaim, "Integration with white folks, yes, even with Jews and Jewesses, but to integrate with Black nobodies, this was carrying things too far" (84–85). Playing it straighter than Killens, Madhubuti delivers the same critique in his 1968 poem "The New Integrationist" by asserting, "I seek integration of negroes with black people" (21).

Other aspects of *The Cotillion* represent obvious verbal links to the author's own earlier efforts. For example, the frequent use of the phrase "Black and comely" to describe Yoruba is a twist, first used in *'Sippi,* on the biblical "black, but comely."[5] In this respect the novel can also be seen as companion and counterpart to one composed at almost exactly the same time, Toni Morrison's *The Bluest Eye.* Although the authors share a fundamental thesis, namely, that standards of beauty made pervasive by the dominant image machine often damage the self-esteem of African Americans, the resolution of the Morrison novel, given Pecola's insanity, is much more grim, an ending possible in the context of the novel because the Breedloves are incapable of providing the support and guidance (and thus the bitter irony of their names) to Pecola that the Lovejoys (whose name is apropos) can for Yoruba.

The Cotillion stands as one of Killens's most successful books. It proved commercially viable, received critical acclaim, and was nominated for the Pulitzer. The plot, as Addison Gayle notes, is a bit slight, but Killens gets all his licks in, explaining his poetic license in the foreword by means of Lumumba. Having experienced the "downtown white workshops" that stifled his creativity, the narrator makes a calculated decision to ignore their advice about craft: "I will intrude, protrude, obtrude or exclude my point of view any time it suits my disposition" (6). Of course, those familiar with Killens's prose, and with the rhetorical nature of prose in general, already knew this.

chapter 5

MoreHeroes

At the same time that he was composing *The Cotillion*, Killens was exploring other literary avenues for advancing his Black heroism project. The novels *Slaves, Great Gittin' Up Morning, A Man Ain't Nothin' but a Man*, and *Great Black Russian* all stem from this period. None has received much critical attention. *Slaves* is a novelization, *Great Gittin' Up Morning* and *A Man Ain't Nothin' but a Man* are usually classified as young adult stories, and *Great Black Russian* was passed over by commercial publishers. Nonetheless, they manifest many of the traits typical of Killens's more celebrated works and thus contribute to a coherent view of his rhetoric and poetics.

Slaves actually appeared before *The Cotillion*, being published in 1969. A film tie-in to the motion picture of the same title (in which Stephen Boyd, Ossie Davis, and Dionne Warwick starred), the novel details the events that lead to a slave insurrection. As a reviewer correctly noted in *Publishers Weekly*, *Slaves* "reads like the black answer to *Mandingo*" (99). But this comment was not an endorsement. The notion seemed to be that Killens counters a simplistic, psychologically underdeveloped tale of Black sexual animals lusting more after whites than after freedom by offering an equally simplistic, psychologically underdeveloped tale of slaves obsessed only with freedom. Perhaps so. However, such countering was considered a strong literary move among, say, some proponents of the Black Aesthetic. They would support an expanded fictional treatment, regardless of how stylized, of the point that Killens had been making all along, that is, the main preoccupation of slaves was emancipation, not lust for whites or servile adaptation to the fact of enslavement. *Slaves* furthers his project, begun in *Youngblood,* to render Southern experience with his sense of historical accuracy.

The plot is a slim one. Because of impending financial ruin, Mr. Stillwell separates Luke from his family and sells him, along with his sidekick Jericho. They end up on a cotton plantation in Mississippi owned by Nathan Mackay, and labor under physically harsher conditions than had existed on the Stillwell horse farm in Kentucky. Nonetheless, Luke's pride and spirit are never broken, even by beating, in the way his master sees fit. Eventually, spurred on by the birth of a girl he helped to deliver, whom he named after his wife, Luke plots an escape, and enlists the aid of Jericho. They plan to take along Cassy, who is Mackay's longstanding but now rebellious mistress, Evaline, his recent purchase, and the baby girl. The plan is discovered and, although the others actually do escape, Luke is killed by Mackay. But despite the simple plot and beyond the generally accepted evil of enslavement, there are ethical issues at the heart of the story worth pondering.

As the novel opens, Luke, the head slave on the Stillwell farm, is returning to Kentucky after being sent by his master to Ohio on a business mission. Luke voluntarily returns from the North to the South, a decision that puzzles his friend Jericho, who dubs him the "slavest slave of all" (11). Luke's decision to forgo his best chance at freedom is even questioned by his wife, Esther, who feels that Luke has acted irresponsibly, family ties notwithstanding. Luke's rationale for his return is that his "kindly" master has promised to manumit him and his family. His mistake lies in not reckoning that the master's economic self-interest would supersede so-called good intentions. So Luke is separated from his family anyway. Having blown his chance at freedom in the North, he is separated from them in slavery.

A second issue involves the slave's view of the sanctity of Black life under slavery. Cassy, as Sethe later would in *Beloved,* kills her own child rather than have it grow up a slave. Years later, after a decade as Stillwell's house mistress, her senses dulled by a steady supply of rum, she has not relented in her view, at least not during the early stages of the novel. She shows no sympathy toward baby

Esther, who happens to be Mackay's daughter. She sees no point
in the birth.

Slaves also represents Killens's fullest commentary on Christianity. He recognizes that Christianity is the most powerful system of values and beliefs among African Americans, so he chooses
to encode his appeals for resistance inside a revolutionary interpretation of the Scriptures. Indeed, the rhetoric of and about
Christianity serves as the binding structural element. Just as the
gospel of Matthew (as in Lovejoy) appears in condensed form in
The Cotillion, the evolving gospel of Luke (as in Stillwell) is central to Slaves. Although ironically, like Matt Lovejoy, Luke bears
a New Testament name, his stance toward the Bible shifts from
a more passive read to a rebellious one aligned more, at least in
Killens's thinking, with the Old Testament.[1] At the outset of the
novel, Luke takes solace in the fact that he lives on a so-called
Christian plantation. All the Stillwell slaves have been baptized.
Luke does not see as does Jericho (walls come tumbling down)
that slavery is wrong in the absolute and is always to be opposed
actively. Jericho believes that if the basic message is to be sub-
servient, then the God in the Bible is the Massa's God. When
Luke recalls that the Bible says "Servant, obey your master," Jericho rejoins that "If the Good Book say that, I don't need to learn
to read" (22). As noted earlier, Luke's obedience is for naught, for
Mr. Stillwell's so-called faith crumbles under economic pressure.
As Mrs. Stillwell protests the sale of slaves, reminding her husband that as Christians they promised never to sell slaves to the
South, Mr. Stillwell replies, "Christianity is one thing—slavery
is something else altogether. . . . I have no intention of having
my son come home from college to find I've let them take Stillwell Farms away from him" (20–21). Although Jericho would
have Luke renounce the Bible at that point, arguing that it is
the wrong JuJu for them, Luke takes his Bible with him when
they are shipped off to New Orleans. Several weeks later, on a
Sunday morning, with church bells ringing all over the city as
backdrop, Luke and Jericho are auctioned, along with Evaline, to
Mackay.

Mackay makes no pretense at being Christian. As he puts it, "I don't believe in villainy or virtue. Only in reality" (40). When he interrogates Luke back at his plantation, he asks Luke about his Bible and about Mrs. Stillwell's teaching him to read. Then Mackay remarks sarcastically, "Taught you to read, gave you the Bible, then took and sold you down the river. That's a Christian for you. . . . Here. I'm giving you the Bible too, but *I'm* going to keep you, Understand?" (47).

Even as the everyday backbreaking labor and repression of life on the Mackay plantation set in, Luke lies awake at night thinking wistfully about the past, not fruitfully confronting his present circumstances:

> It was a bad dream that he was dreaming and he would soon wake up in his neat little cabin with Esther in his arms and the children in their beds and old Massa and ol' Missus in the Big House, Kindly Christian people, and God was good and just and worked in mysterious ways but performed his wonders in due time, and Massa would keep his promise and set Luke free, the Lord looked out for his Chosen people. Wake up, Luke! He tried his damneddest to wake up from this nightmare. Wake up, Luke! Wake up, Luke and stop your dreaming and face this nightmare of reality. (56)

Only when Luke's faith evolves to the point where he can be as realistic as Mackay does he stand a chance of changing his condition. Jericho has insisted all along that if they are to embrace God, they must also embrace the idea, as generations of African Americans have been taught, that God helps those who help themselves.

While Luke is recovering from a brutal beating administered by overseers, he begins to gravitate more toward the Old Testament, in particular the story of Moses leading the Israelites from bondage. Luke doubts that he could be a Moses, but he views the birth of baby Esther as a providential sign and vows to make a good life for her somehow. Luke is further motivated after he works a party at the Big House. Like Daphne in *The Cotillion*, Luke is profoundly moved by a conversation he overhears that dispels any notions he still retained about a master's intentions. He hears Mackay lecture to his friends: "I took artists, sculptors, and turned them into niggers. And you got to keep them niggers twenty-four hours a day. You got to make them believe deep down in their hearts and souls they're niggers. The moment they stop thinking of themselves as niggers, you're in trouble. I wouldn't tolerate slaves on my farm that wouldn't call each other nigger" (95).[2] Later that night, down in the slave quarters, Luke acknowledges that Jericho has in fact been a true Christian all along because he never tried to be a "good nigger" and never believed in "good massas." "You a Christian," Luke tells him, "cause you always knew slavery was the Devil's workhouse, and you always worked to bring the building down" (101). In this spirit of understanding and brotherhood, the insurrection is planned. Unfortunately, Luke becomes a martyr, but baby Esther, with Jericho, Cassy, and Evaline, do leave the plantation with the help of several slaves and white sympathizer Mrs. Bennett. As in his other novels, Killens defines success for African Americans, even that laced with tragedy, as resulting from communal action and belief in common ideals. If Christianity is to be prominent among those ideals, then Killens clearly aims to promote a Christianity that is revolutionary.

Several other aspects link *Slaves* to Killens's other fiction. Jericho is the resident folk wit. Luke is cast physically in the Youngblood-Chaney-Lumumba mode, "tall and straight and handsome-black" (7). Cassy imagines him as a tall, Black, handsome Ashanti warrior, a man of supreme dignity. It is this image, this fearlessness, that awakens feelings of love and admiration in her. Cassy herself is described much like Yoruba Lovejoy: "Black and comely. . . . She was lovely, she was statuesque and queenly" (46). Cassy is sustained in part by the collection of African masks, a link to the African past, that is kept in the Big House.

The premises in *Slaves* are restated with even greater force in Killens's 1972 adolescent novel, *Great Gittin' Up Morning*. The plot also revolves, naturally, around a slave insurrection, in this case Denmark Vesey's famous attempt at revolution in South Carolina. Vesey, in fact, managed to mobilize more than one thousand slaves to participate in a rebellion to take place in Charleston on June 16, 1822.[3] But perhaps the most intriguing aspect of the revolt to Killens was Vesey's status: a fairly prosperous free man even though his wife and children were slaves. Thus Killens is able to portray a hero whose love for family and brethren, and absolute hatred of American slavery, compels him to arms despite his own relatively secure status. Vesey is a more compelling figure than the equivocating though ultimately heroic Luke. Vesey already has what Luke and the others seek, namely freedom, and risks it in an attempt to liberate masses of Blacks.

Details of Vesey's early life are sketchy, and Killens takes the novelist's license to create events and character, such as predictably casting Vesey as uncommonly handsome and imposing as are all his male protagonists up to that point. However, the latter parts of the novel are quite faithful to the historical record and to Vesey's character and temperament as a Talented Tenth role model. The fifty-five-year-old Vesey is described as critically literate and extremely well read. And as in many African-American stories, including several by Killens, we see the explicit connection between Black literacy and Black liberation:

> Denmark read everything he could get his hands on—
> newspapers, books, periodicals, magazines. He had a reading
> acquaintance with the abolitionist movement, the antislavery
> movement Quakers, the Underground Railroad. . . . He
> kept up with the debates in the United States Congress.
> He had read antislavery pamphlets smuggled into town by
> seamen. He knew the U.S. Constitution and the Declaration
> of Independence and the Bill of Rights. He could recite each
> one verbatim. The more he read, the more he heard from
> the mouths of seamen, the more he overheard from Haitian
> refugees, the more bitter was the pill of slavery for this proud
> Black man to swallow. (10–11)

This depiction of Vesey probably derives from one provided by historian John Lofton in *Insurrection in South Carolina*.[4]

Although Denmark Vesey was a great man, it is not a great man theory of history that produces him in Killens's novel. The author recognizes the relative prosperity of Blacks in Charleston and the unusual mobility that slaves in the area enjoyed. Because the city was an important commercial port, there was great demand for artisan labor such as carpenters (as Vesey was), blacksmiths, mechanics, and lumberyard workers. Blacks vastly outnumbered working-class whites (as well as whites overall); thus, they were the major part of the workforce. Slaveowners hired out their slaves, many of whom were skilled, with the bulk of the wages earned going to the masters. This arrangement was generally more profitable than using those slaves to pick cotton. So, ironically, it was the slaveowners' greed that helped establish the fluid community in which the idea of insurrection would take hold. The fact of this historical development supported Killens's belief that slaves, as well as truly conscious and committed free Blacks, were in general not appeased by halfway measures. Vesey, therefore, was supported by numerous co-conspirators who were also free men or relatively privileged slaves, such as Ned and Rolla Bennett, the governor's own servants.

Killens extends the commentary about liberatory religion embedded in *Slaves*. Vesey "preached freedom and liberation right out of the Holy Bible" (61). Like Luke Stillwell, Killens's Vesey gravitates toward the story of Moses, positing that God would turn on Blacks if they do not attempt to liberate themselves. Justifying his decision not to spare women or children during the planned rebellion, Vesey quotes Joshua 6:21, "and they utterly destroyed all that was in the city, both man and woman, young and old, and ox, and sheep, and ass, with the edge of the sword" (63–64). Down to the particular citing of the Scriptures, this passage is historically accurate. But for Killens, Christianity has no automatically privileged place among religious rituals, as indicated by his description of the conspirators on the verge of action. "Some had engaged in voodoo rites all night long the night before. Some prayed to the

Christian god, Jehovah, others prayed to the god of Islam, Allah, before whom there was no other. Some prayed to three or four gods simultaneously" (101–2). Killens's concern is not with a particular deity; any god is fine who sanctions Black revolution.

The rebellion is ultimately thwarted. One hundred seventeen Blacks are charged as a result; of that number seventy-nine are put on trial. Thirty-four are hanged, including all the principal leaders except Monday Gell, who turns informant. Thirty-nine of the convicted and many of the innocent are exiled from the state. Laws subsequently passed by the state legislature include one that bars Blacks who leave the state from returning; another requires that after June 1, 1823, every free Black over fifteen years of age have a white guardian who would be legally responsible for him.

At Vesey's trial, witnesses who testified against him, like William Paul and George Wilson, argued that Vesey had misused the Bible to foment an uprising. The presiding judge, Lionel H. Kennedy, in pronouncing sentence, declared (and Killens takes this from the actual trial report):

> In addition to treason, you have committed the grossest impiety, in attempting to pervert the sacred words of God and torture them into a sanction for the crimes of the blackest hue. It is evident, that you are totally insensible of the divine influence of that Gospel, "all of whose paths lead to peace." It was to reconcile us to our destinies on earth, and to enable us to discharge with fidelity, all the duties of life, that those holy precepts were imparted by heaven to fallen man.
>
> If you had searched them with sincerity, you would have discovered instructions, immediately applicable to the deluded victims of your artful wiles—"Servants (says Saint Paul) obey in all things your masters, according to the flesh, not with eye-service, as men-pleasers, but in the singleness of heart, fearing God." And then again, "Servants (says Saint Peter) be subject to your masters with all fear, not only to the good and gentle, but also to the forward." (*Great Gittin' Up Morning* 123–24; *The Trial Record of Denmark Vesey* 136)

For Killens's Vesey, however, his own take on the Bible is correct. As he thinks to himself in the courtroom, "[T]he master and the slave would never have identical interpretations" (125).

Killens turns to another familiar icon in his 1975 adolescent novel *A Man Ain't Nothin' but a Man*, a book based on John Henry, the legendary steel driver who reportedly worked for the Chesapeake and Ohio Railroad in the 1870s on the dangerous Big Bend tunnel project in West Virginia. He has been the source of numerous songs and tales. The most common versions, as well as most tame, are that John Henry, a former slave, was a proud and stubborn man who pitted his enormous strength and ability against a steam drill in an attempt to delay mechanization. Although John Henry won the contest, he died when it was over from a stroke or heart attack. The fundamental structure of any John Henry tale derives from the basic ballad, more accurately termed a matrix of ballads. As identified by Norm Cohen, there are five elements:

1. an infantile premonition,
2. preparation for the contest (including the challenge, a financial incentive, John Henry's request for hammers of a specific weight, and the like),
3. the contest itself (usually limited to such information as who stood where, how rapidly each contestant drove, John Henry's comments as the contest proceeded, and praise for John Henry's powerful strokes),
4. the hero's last words, death, and burial, and
5. much editorializing on his woman (the clothes she wore, her behavior at his funeral, sometimes her own steel-driving prowess) (72)

All the details that would make up a lengthy narrative have been subjected to the interpretation of various storytellers, including the specific motivation for the contest, how John Henry obtained his freedom, the nature of his personality, his relationship to his family and home, whether he had a son or not, whether his main love interest was Lucy or Polly Ann, whether he was married, what feats of heroism were performed, the margin of his victory over the steam drill, the length of the contest, and even where he was born (he's been claimed by every state in the South).

As a boy growing up in Georgia, Killens undoubtedly heard a variety of John Henry songs and stories. He probably became aware at some point of the version published in the *Messenger* in 1925 by A. Philip Randolph and Chandler Owen. In their version, John Henry receives his freedom because he saves his master from drowning, not an action Killens would advocate. John Henry and his former master are described as best friends, yet John Henry's girlfriend, Lucy, remains enslaved on the plantation. Therefore, John Henry is largely motivated to work in order to purchase Lucy's freedom from someone who is supposed to be his best friend. Randolph and Owen do portray John Henry as "pure Negro" and deem him noble, but his facial features are described as ugly. The showdown with the steam drill is to help his master win a $500 bet, of which John Henry is promised $50. When Captain Walters informs a dying John Henry that they won the contest, John Henry affirms in third-person plural, "We've beat him" (75).

Perhaps the dominant John Henry story by the 1970s, as W. Nikola-Lisa suggests, was Ezra Jack Keats's *John Henry: An American Legend*. Keats's tale is not political with respect to the African-American community. As Nikola-Lisa notes: "John Henry's death symbolizes for Keats the waning of the prized American ideal of individualism. It is in this respect that Keats' John Henry gains widespread appeal, but at the price of ignoring the underlying racial tension inherent in the conflict between John Henry, an ex-slave, and white railroad bosses notorious for their exploitation of black laborers" (54). Killens was likely aware of the Keats version as well. The episode where John Henry saves the lives of a work crew by bravely preventing an explosion probably is drawn from that source. But as Brett Williams asserts, "Killens' John Henry is clearly a black hero and a laboring hero. He does not represent dumb brute strength, but rather links his contest with the machine drill to human dignity" (93).

Killens's John Henry thus evokes memories of Joe and Robby Youngblood although in real time, of course, John Henry was one of the models that shaped the Youngblood males. At any rate, like the Youngbloods and most of the writer's characters, his John Henry never learns to "grin and bow and scrape and take low in front of white folks" (18). Although the notion of being a steel driver, like his father, has been on John Henry's mind from the time he was a toddler, he actually chooses the vocation because it pays significantly higher wages than picking cotton on the plantation or rousting cotton on the waterfront. As such, the job increases the prospects that he and his wife, Polly Anne, can purchase a farm. As he explains to her: "We done worked on somebody else's land all our natcherl born days, and I'm working for the day to come when we can work our own soil and for our own selves and our chilluns. That's what I'm looking forward to. That's what freedom got to mean to all us Black folks. . . . Our own sweet black earth. Freedom don't mean nothin' if it don't mean that" (75–76). That all political power is based on the ownership of land, that it is the basis of nation building, has been, of course, a key principle of Black nationalist discourse.

On the other hand, what does not fit easily into Black nationalist discourse are the images of fellowship involving John Henry, Uncle Buddy, Ben Lawson, a white coworker, and the Chinese-American worker George Ling Lee. As a group they regularly dine at John Henry's home. Notwithstanding, ethnic differences do remain, and they are exploited by Captain Joe Brad, who spreads racist rumors to drive a wedge between the workers. Only Polly Anne's intervention keeps a confrontation between John Henry and Ben Lawson from becoming tragic. As they all afterward talk in Ben Lawson's home, John Henry discusses the limitation of ethnic alliances, telling Lawson that "when it come down to a test where a man really live at, you a white man first and a good man afterwards" (151). Lawson vehemently denies the charge, eventually arguing that he treats all men fairly regardless of color. He blames one of the captain's instigators, Will Hodge, for the trouble and plans to shoot him. John Henry counters by interceding, and he explains that Will Hodge is but a pawn being used by management. The more the men talk and understand management's tactics, the more the story turns back toward a transethnic leftist awareness reminiscent of portions of *Youngblood, And Then We Heard the Thunder,* and *Black Man's Burden.* John Henry, Uncle Buddy, Lawson, and Lee understand, a lesson Killens himself recalls from his union organizing days, how racism is employed to undermine working-class solidarity, with the result that management increases the profit margin at the expense of workers' well-being. As they wind up their session, John Henry reminds the others, "[J]ust remember, a man ain't nothin' but a man, don't care what color he be. It seem such a hard thing to remember, especially hard for the poor white working folks" (154).

A popular song version recorded by Harry Belafonte, to whom Killens's novel is in fact dedicated, expresses the same sentiment about manhood:

> John Henry said to his Captain,
> "A man ain't nothin' but a man,
> And before I'll let your steam drill beat me down
> Gonna die with my hammer in my hand, Lord, Lord,
> Gonna die with my hammer in my hand."

The lyrics Killens uses in his novel are more explicit concerning ethnicity:

> A man ain't nothin' but a man—
> A man ain't nothin' but a man.
> He can be white or Black,
> He can be yellow or tan,
> It makes no difference when it's man to man.
> It's been like that since the world began.
> A man ain't nothin' but a man. (24)

By the time we get to the climactic challenge, the story is more complicated than the usual John Henry tale because of the merger of Black nationalist and broader leftist sentiments. In order to prevent cuts in wages or layoffs, John Henry tries to prove that a full complement of men is more economically expedient than machines. He feels a particular responsibility to save jobs for Black workers, knowing that other job prospects for them almost always mean a return to some plantation and a menial existence. After he wins the contest by drilling ten inches deeper than the drill, and presumably saves the jobs, he admits, facing his death, that mechanization is inevitable. In his view, the enemy is not machines, the unwise use of them is. The implied line of reasoning, of course, is that if economic inequality that damages Blacks were to persist, then that would constitute evidence that machines were indeed being misused.

Williams labels *A Man Ain't Nothin' but a Man* the best of the popular fiction about John Henry. While faithful to the Cohen outline, Killens writes an unusually political, family-oriented tale. In addition, he breaks the cycle of tragedy often indicated in the ballads. As Williams writes of John Henry, "Often he addresses his last words to this child, and often he warns the boy that he too will die a steel-driving man" (124). In the Killens story the child has yet to be born and its sex is unknown. Beyond that, John Henry has agreed with Polly Anne that if they have a son he would not become a steel driver. "I wants him to be a doctor or a schoolteacher, a leader of the people or something like that whatsonever he be" (127). Here is another Du Boisian, Talented Tenth twist to a Killens novel. Thus Polly Anne does not demonstrate any steel-driving prowess at the close of the novel, as is the case in many other versions of the tale. She makes no attempt to replicate John Henry's life, but by picking up his hammer she does intend to feel his strength and goodness as a source of inspiration: "And understood she must be strong. For their unborn child. And for the things for which he fought and died. And for all the future generations" (176).

Killens's last published novel, *Great Black Russian: A Novel on the Life and Times of Alexander Pushkin*, was also directly inspired by Harry Belafonte, who suggested in the 1960s that a biographical treatment of Pushkin could be a viable film project. Killens began the background research, became hooked on the subject, and for well over a decade studied materials about the man generally considered the greatest of all Russian poets. Unfortunately, the novel (the movie never happened) was not published until 1989, two years after the author's death.

There are several reasons Killens would be enamored of Pushkin. He was a poet in a culture where writers could achieve great fame and stature. He was a vernacular artist who spoke, unlike many of his French-worshipping predecessors, in the voice of the Russian masses. He wrote in support of revolutionary causes. Obviously, however, the irresistable attraction was Pushkin's African ancestry, thus the chance to portray in fiction another Black hero. Addison Gayle writes of Killens in the introduction to the novel:

> He is, like Pushkin, "the people's poet," one for whom
> concern with people is more important than wealth or
> fame. It is this concern which enables both him and the
> subject whose life he carefully researched and ably presented
> in fiction to remain vibrant forces in the daily lives of
> revolutionaries/romantics everywhere. When he visited
> Moscow and was taken on a tour which included the shrine
> to Pushkin, he stood looking down at the crypt of this black
> Russian poet. At that moment, two centuries of history
> merged and one poet reached across the vast expanse of time
> and distance to embrace another. (13)

Pushkin's great-grandfather on his mother's side was Ibrahim Hannibal, also known as the Negro of Peter the Great. This fact is highlighted throughout the first quarter of the novel—with both negative and positive connotations. As the elder Pushkin argues with his son and tries to persuade the budding poet to stop writing poems in Russian as opposed to French, he cruelly refers to young Pushkin as "you little African bastard!" (39). As his mother scolds young Pushkin to be more like his little brother and sister, who incidentally do not look Africoid, she remarks that "he just has the devil in him. It's his African blood rising up in him" (43). Positive comments about his African heritage come from his grandmother. Referring to Hannibal, using a favorite Killens description, she allows that "he was so tall and Black and comely" (47). On several occasions, suffering from stress and loneliness, Pushkin himself conjures up visions of Hannibal, who apparently enjoyed a distinguished career in Czar Peter's court. The first apparition occurs when Pushkin (also known as Sasha) is a student at the Lyceum, which he attended between the ages of twelve and eighteen. As Pushkin lies on his bed after a talk with his grandmother, "the tall Black man with dark eyes that seemed to pierce the darkness with their intensity came to his bedside and talked with him about times gone by, when he himself was a boy in far away Africa, a young Ethiopian prince" (77). Shortly thereafter, Pushkin declares to a schoolmate, a point he repeats on several occasions, "I'm an African-Russian. . . . A Russian with an African descendancy" (79).

Killens provides what is perhaps the most "African read" possible of Pushkin's life given the available data. He is joined in this effort by Gayle, who, depicting Pushkin, writes of the "overwhelming impact made upon him by his African ancestor" (Introduction 11). Gayle also credits Ibrahim Hannibal with much of Pushkin's moral development as the "poet who loved human freedom and who despised chains and shackles everywhere" (11). However, it can be argued, and many have, that Pushkin was far more Russian than anything else. Nor could Killens seriously dispute that claim, a point he conceded during a 1983 interview with Kenneth Peeples. It ought to be noted as well that the Pushkin name, traceable to the early fifteenth century, was one of the oldest among the nobility in Russia, and although Pushkin was indeed fascinated with his Ethiopian ties, he was also proud of his father's lineage. He named his younger son Grigorii after the first known male in the Pushkin line. But Killens, defending his strong Africanist rendering, emphasized that Pushkin acknowledged and took pride in his African heritage. This is certainly true as indicated by the fact that Pushkin left behind an unfinished novel titled *The Negro of Peter the Great*. Additionally, that sense of pride apparently influenced his views on the plight of fellow Blacks, including those enslaved in the West. Avrahm Yarmolinsky notes that Pushkin spoke on at least one occasion of "my brother Negroes" (14). It would be hard, though, to credit Hannibal, who owned a thousand slaves according to Killens himself, with his great-grandson's antislavery sentiment. The more immediate source was always before him— millions of peasants and serfs whose suffering was understood and detested by a sensitive and sympathetic artist.

So Pushkin is not solely a Black hero, but he is enough of one to fit easily among the Killens line of protagonists. He resembles Luke Stillwell, for example, when he argues that he is morally right to deceive oppressive rulers. To recall part of the climactic scene in *Slaves*:

> Mackay said, "You were lying through your teeth, weren't you, Boy?"
>
> Luke pondered the master's words, then said, in a trembly voice, "Man, I don't owe you the truth." (131)

During his meeting with Nicholas, Pushkin remembers how he had once replied to a fellow student who chided him for lying to the authorities: "There are Imperial truths and there are gospel truths, and they are just about the same, mostly lies. . . . Then there are truths that liberate the people, which are altogether different. I do not owe the Imperial Court the people's truth. All I owe it is damnation and exposure" (266).

Pushkin also favors a host of Killens characters, stretching all the way back to Big Mama in *Youngblood*, when he instructs a serf, Olga Kalasnikova, never to love her master, even if it is he. He is not to be admired for impregnating the woman, but he does sign manumission papers to set her free in the days following their most important conversation. As Olga expresses love and a desire to remain his serf girl, Pushkin instructs her that "you must learn to hate your master, sweet woman. You want to be free, don't you?" (230).

Pushkin was not a thoroughly committed and uncompromising rebel like Denmark Vesey, yet his influence was profound, an impact Killens understood well. To the extent that Russian workers read any poetry, it was Pushkin's that they read. Subversives were often caught with copies of his poems in their possession. Masses of people responded favorably to poems like his "Ode to Freedom."[5] Such writing and other agitation led to his being exiled by Czar Alexander.

In terms of concrete political acts, Pushkin is best known as the "Bard of the Decembrists." After the death of Czar Alexander in 1825, his brother Nicholas ascended to the throne. A rebellion was planned for December 14 but was crushed by the emperor's Horse Guards. Five members of the group, which became known as the Decembrists, were hanged and several others banished to Siberia. Many were Pushkin's friends and, in fact, had been inspired by him. The following year, Pushkin was summoned from his exile in Mikhailovskoye by Nicholas for a face-to-face meeting at the conclusion of which Nicholas announced a "new" Pushkin. The next eleven years, the last of his life, were spent in an uneasy relationship with the czar.

Ironically, though he is indeed born of nobility, Killens's Pushkin is less noble than his other tragic heroes. Despite his genius and impact, he is a brooding, often depressed talent, who spends far too much time dissipating, playing cards, and being complicit in the exploitation of serfs. He is the product of a decadent family that has no particular commitment to social justice. He dies at the age of thirty-seven, not mortally wounded in the fight against racism and economic exploitation, but as the result of a duel fought because of a love affair between his wife and the Frenchman George Charles d'Anthes. Nor is he anywhere near the Killens physical prototype at a diminutive five-feet-four inches, with "sallow jaundiced" skin (17).[6] Yet he was of African descent and, in general, valiantly for the people.

Yarmolinsky thinks that Alexander Pushkin is best understood as a poet who, "though not a man of the masses, felt with them by reason of his deep humanity, and had their emancipation at heart" (13). Those qualities—and Ibrahim—are his ticket into the Killens pantheon.

chapter 6

Ideology and Writers' Conferences

A serious survey of the impact of John Oliver Killens on public discourse must include attention to the literary conferences he organized. They function as "texts" that amplify his views on literary politics. This is not to suggest that Killens could script any of the conference participants. Sophisticated and articulate on their own, they capably spoke for themselves, sometimes, in turn, influencing Killens. The point, however, is that Killens generally knew who could be counted on to deliver messages he favored; therefore, the conferences largely functioned as elaborate sets of testimonials. It is in this sense that novelist Arthur Flowers, a Killens protégé, likes warmly to regard him as an "ideological orchestrator."[1] On the other hand, one can hardly help but recall the dim view of such orchestration expressed by Harold Cruse, who, referring specifically to a 1965 conference directed by Killens, wrote that "Negro Writers Conferences settle nothing, solve nothing, pose nothing, analyze nothing, plan nothing, create nothing—not even a decent new literary review—which is the least any bunch of serious, self-respecting writers with a gripe ought to do" (*Crisis of the Negro Intellectual* 498). Cruse does allow that at the 1965 conference, he heard papers that were "informative, eloquent, and pointed" (501). One should suppose that a paper that is informative demonstrates at the very least a posing of some sort, likely involves a modicum of analysis, and potentially resolves some issues or ambiguities as well. It is true that these affairs do not put to rest great cultural questions, no more than a church resolves everyone's moral dilemmas because services happen to be held. For example, utter repudiation of socialist realism in exchange for a strict Black nationalist aesthetic or detailed proposals for building a Black cultural infrastructure, items that supposedly were on Cruse's agenda, obviously cannot be treated with finality at such affairs.

While one can certainly sympathize with Cruse's frustration concerning the immediately generative limitations of conferences, the Killens record on developing cultural mechanisms is actually impressive. The Harlem Writers Guild, which he co-founded in 1950, remains an important workshop more than fifty years later and currently operates out of the Schomburg Center for Research in Black Culture. Its members—ranging from the late John Henrik Clarke to Maya Angelou to Terry McMillan to Walter Mosley—have produced literally hundreds of books. In addition to workshop activities, the guild sponsors outreach activities in venues such as libraries and schools to promote African-American literature. Some of the growth and success of the guild has to be attributed to Killens's high profile as a literary organizer, an element that was part and parcel of the writers' conferences he directed. In addition, Killens was a member of the collective that founded *Freedomways: A Quarterly Review of the Negro Freedom Movement*, which was one of the more notable journals founded in the 1960s and which largely served as a publishing outlet for the Harlem Writers Guild.[2] Although not strictly a literary organ, *Freedomways* featured creative writing and literary reviews (all of Killens's major books were reviewed) because its founders were extremely interested in the relation of the arts to the Black freedom struggle.[3] Writers whose work appeared in the journal include Alex Haley, Alice Walker, Pablo Neruda, Derek Walcott, Mari Evans, Langston Hughes, Sterling Brown, James Baldwin, Gwendolyn Brooks, Nikki Giovanni, Arna Bontemps, and June Jordan.

Writers conferences, while not perfect, can and in fact do serve as important vehicles of inspiration and cultural diffusion. Attendance now numbers in the thousands at the occasional Black Writers Conferences convened at Medgar Evers College, where Killens sparked the inaugural meeting in 1986.[4] An annual conference, a goal of Killens, has been conducted since 1991 by Haki

Madhubuti, whose first national exposure came at an event led by
Killens in 1968.[5]

Despite whatever shortcomings, then, the conferences Killens
spearheaded between 1965 and 1986 remain a noteworthy contribution and are important milestones in Black literary history.
The focus here is on the major lines of argument, developed by
both Killens and several key panelists, which bind the occasions
into a coherent whole.

Killens's affinity and agenda for writers' conferences can be
traced back to one sponsored in 1959 by the American Society of African Culture (AMSAC). The theme was "The American Negro Writer and His Roots," and the author sat as chairman of the planning committee, which included William Branch,
John Henrik Clarke, Julian Mayfield, Loften Mitchell, and Sarah
Wright. In addition to the members of the planning group, panelists included Samuel Allen, Arna Bontemps, Arthur P. Davis,
Langston Hughes, and J. Saunders Redding. In his own paper, Killens sounded a theme most urgent to him, that is, the production
of positive, optimistic, affirming Black literature. He also outlined
the following five-point proposal to be presented to the general
body of AMSAC, a proposal to provide incentives for African-
American authors:

1. The establishment of an annual award for creative writing
   in the area of Negro life.
2. The establishment of annual grants to send one or more
   Negro writers to Africa for a period of six months or longer,
   with the hope that they may be inspired to write a novel or
   a play on some aspect of this gigantic subject.
3. The establishment of a theatre for producing and
   encouraging plays on Negro life.
4. The publication of a periodical for Negro writers and for
   material about the Negro.
5. The establishment of an annual conference for Negro
   writers. ("Opportunities for Development of Negro Talent"
   70)

The last point, of course, is the one in which Killens would invest the most energy. AMSAC did not establish an annual conference, nor could he. But he pursued the idea doggedly and staged major conferences whenever he could command the necessary resources.

The 1965 conference, titled "The Negro Writer's Vision of America," was held at the New School for Social Research, where Killens served as writer-in-residence. Held in April, three months after the death of Lorraine Hansberry, the gathering was convened in honor of the late playwright. Panelists included John Henrik Clarke, Ossie Davis, Sarah Wright, Loften Mitchell, LeRoi Jones, and James Baldwin, all of whom shared amicable experiences with Killens.[6] A conspicuous development was that Ralph Ellison, who had an adversarial relationship with Killens dating back to Killens's review of *Invisible Man* in 1952, declined to attend. To expect Ellison to participate—and Cruse is right on this score—was unreasonable given the aesthetic and political bent of Killens and his associates in the Harlem Writers Guild, who formed the main strand of the event. Furthermore, critical remarks subsequently made at the conference, primarily by John Henrik Clarke and white historian Herbert Aptheker, practically assured that Ellison would never attend a gathering where Killens was at the helm. Clarke, for instance, in a response to positive comments about Ellison made by NAACP Labor Secretary Herbert Hill, asserted:

> I hope Mr. Hill can be brief with this exaggeration of the role of Ralph Ellison who has spent so much time in the last ten years in flight from his own people and has not even answered most mail addressed to him by his fellow black writers and has said positively that art and literature are not racial. He won't come into any Afro-American writer's conference. I think Ellison wrote one very interesting thing. From the point of view of craftsmanship it was a very good and powerful work. Whether Ralph Ellison will follow up, whether Ralph Ellison has grown up is open to question in many quarters starting with me. (qtd. in *The Crisis of the Negro Intellectual* 507)

Aptheker added the opinion regarding Ellison that "in terms of what he has published and also his published assertions, he has made himself rather not particularly visible in the struggles of the Negro people" (508).

Although Clarke was particularly harsh on Ellison (Killens had softened his stance by then), it must be noted that criticism of Ellison was not isolated.[7] He was often received with hostility by African-American college students. Even if Clarke, as well as Killens, had been absent from the New School event, it is unlikely that Ellison, had he participated, would have been embraced by many in the audience, which consisted largely of Black cultural nationalists and old-line leftists.

Of the writers present at the conference, James Baldwin was the one who received the most attention, both positive and negative. He held the audience in suspense with his keynote address but by the end of the conference had been labeled, according to Gay Talese, "an extremely talented literary prostitute" by conferee Myrna Baines, who was reportedly on the staff of *National Review*, the conservative publication edited by William Buckley (26). However, for present purposes, the crucial aspect of the appearance of Baldwin, the star invitee, is the degree to which his rhetoric compared and contrasted to that of Killens. To be sure, the two had different artistic visions. One can imagine Killens, who invariably stressed Black nobility and heroism, cringing as Baldwin announced that "I modeled myself on the junkies and whores because they form my background" and that "my history began on the auction block." As Killens, and Malcolm X, had asserted, "It is important for us to know that our history did not begin with slavery's scars."[8] On the other hand, Baldwin offered a revisionist take on American history and insisted that the moral obligation of artists was to fight for social justice. As described by M. S. Handler of the *New York Times*:

> One of the American tragedies, Mr. Baldwin said in his
> speech, is that the "white people cannot face the lies of their
> own history."

He asserted that the "white Anglo-Saxons" had falsified
the history of the United States and were today prisoners
of their own myth-making. He scathingly spoke of the
earliest settlers that had abandoned Europe out of sheer
poverty or had come out of English jails only to manufacture
"aristocratic" status for themselves in the colonies. "Who," he
asked, "knows anything about the Virginia aristocrats outside
of Virginia?"

Mr. Baldwin continued, "The liberation of the people
of this country, our lowly people, our junkies, and, yes, our
middle class, depends on whether we are able to make a real
confrontation with our history. For you face more terrible
trials before you can emerge from the age of puberty."

All the black artist is trying to do, he told his stunned
audience, is "to make you remember who you really are." (31)

This second strand of Baldwin's presentation suited Killens just
fine. One may even wonder, given the previous interactions between Killens and Baldwin, and recalling once again the col-
laboration between Killens and Malcolm X, how much of Baldwin's speech was directly influenced by the conference director. Or
how responsible was Baldwin for the content of some of Killens's
later speeches? Either way, the emphasis on American history as
a literary and rhetorical battle was often part of Killens's opening remarks at subsequent conferences, including the last one he
organized. As he spoke of history at the National Black Writers
Conference in 1986:

Americans have never been able to face their history, which
is why the American people are inflicted with a Cowboy-
Indian mentality, like the clannish cowboy in the White
House with a mind set that imagines still charging up San
Juan Hill with the white man's burden, with Teddy Roosevelt
with his Big Stick Policy. Think of Manifest Destiny, Monroe
Doctrine, Gun Boat Diplomacy. That's a hell of a lot of
historical distortion to carry around from year to year. It is up

especially to the writer to do the American people a favor and
rub America's nostrils in the dung heap of its history, which is
genocide and murder in the hundred millions of black and red
men and women, and thievery of an entire North American
land mass. That is the history of this country that it has never
faced. Until America faces its history there will continue to
be police actions, Vietnams, Bays of Pigs, Grenada invasions,
overthrows of democratically elected governments such as
in Chile, counterrevolutionary activities in central America,
presidential schizophrenia and on and on.[9]

In "Reverberations from a Writers Conference," Hoyt Fuller,
one of the proponents of the emerging Black Arts Movement,
noted that the 1965 conference reflected "the deepening es-
trangement of the Negro writer from the so-called 'mainstream'
of American literature" (78). In particular, he cited the disparag-
ing remarks made by white critic Richard Gilman, drama critic
for *Newsweek* magazine, and the rebuttal by LeRoi Jones. On a
panel titled "What Negro Playwrights Are Saying," Gilman argued Black playwrights were only in a preliminary stage, a notion
dismissed by Jones and, subsequently, by Fuller as well.[10] For Fuller,
Gilman's comments illustrated a problem faced by Black writers,
artists whose commercial success was often jeopardized because
of unfavorable reviews by white critics. The eventual solution, in
Fuller's view, entailed cultivating a strong relationship between
Black writers and Black audiences. If Black writers turned to their
community, Fuller reasoned, the community would be supportive, forcing a change in the white critical reception, which, in
turn, would lead to a larger readership overall for Black writers.
As Fuller concludes, "Once Negro writers are honored in Harlem,
then the critics will come to Harlem, bringing with them the general public. But this time around, the critics will have accepted
Negro writers on the writers' own terms, and that will make all
the difference" (84). Fuller deemed the conference a success in
terms of popular support and apparently hoped it could spur the
activity he advocated.

By the time the New School conference was held, Killens had accepted a position as writer-in-residence at Fisk University. There he organized conferences in 1966, 1967, and 1968. The 1966 conference was convened around the theme "The Image of the Negro in American Literature." Esteemed social critic J. Saunders Redding, who participated in the AMSAC conference, served as the opening keynote speaker and charged that some African-American writers were developing an inappropriate line of characters, arguing that they were "making heroes out of heels" (Llorens 55). He specifically mentioned John A. Williams, Chester Himes, Rosa Guy, and James Baldwin. The respective works in question were *Night Song, If He Hollers Let Him Go, Bird in My Window,* and *Another Country.* While the remarks proved provocative, and expressed sentiments not wholly shared by Killens, it was evident that the morally upright characters that Killens created met with the approval of Redding, as well as much of the audience, and were his preferred prototypes.

Redding's remarks would not have been surprising to those, like Killens, who were aware of his previous and consistent pronouncements about African-American literature. As far back as 1945, in an essay titled "The Negro Author: His Publisher, His Public and His Purse," Redding criticized the likes of Wallace Thurman (*Blacker the Berry*) and Claude McKay (*Banana Bottom*) for producing "empty, banal, pseudo-exotic tripe that is sometimes taken as the substance of Negro life in America" (146). Similarly, in his 1949 essay "American Negro Literature," he inveighed against negative stereotypes of Blacks reflected in the writing of both Black and white authors.[11] Those ideas were basically restated ten years later, often verbatim, in his address at the AMSAC conference, which was titled "The Negro Writer and His Relationship to His Roots," and in the 1965 *Negro Digest* print symposium, "The Task of the Negro Writer as Artist." Most recently, in the April 1966 issue of *The Crisis,* which was published just before his appearance at Fisk, he reviewed Guy's novel and made the "heroes out of heels" comment that he repeated at the conference. The criticism of Himes was ironic, though, because in the 1949 essay he praised Himes's *If He Hollers Let Him Go* and *Lonely Crusade* as notable literary achievements and examples of successful appeals to both Black and white audiences.

Killens himself sat on the panel titled "The Novel and Its Social Relevance to the Negro Revolution." After stating his familiar claim, inspired by Du Bois, that all art is propaganda, he went on to insist that "our literature should have social relevance to the world struggle and *especially* to the struggle of black Americans" (Llorens 57). In a similar vein, novelist William Melvin Kelley declared that "the task of the Negro writer should differ from that of the white writer in that, among other things, he should be addressing himself to the Negro" (Llorens 64). Overall, ideas about Black consciousness, Black affirmation, and politically useful art—core values to Killens—received considerable play and were compatible with the prevailing mood of the conference attendees.

Perhaps the most inspirational, strategic, and consequential articulation of the identity politics most promoted at the conference was voiced by Melvin B. Tolson. Tolson served partly as a counterpart to the thought and presence of Robert Hayden, the distinguished poet who was a professor at Fisk during Killens's tenure. The relationship between the two faculty members was contentious at best because of institutional decisions and openly expressed disagreements between the two about literary politics. Hayden had been at Fisk for twenty years, had been continually saddled with a heavy teaching load that hampered his poetic productivity, and had covered everything the English Department had demanded of him. Yet he was deprived of opportunities to teach creative writing courses once Killens arrived. Furthermore, Hayden decried Killens's views about art and politics, and he disapproved of how popular those views were among the student body. Maybe mindful of an earlier time when writing by African Americans was sometimes described as "okay for a Negro," Hayden characteristically referred to himself as a poet who only happened to be Negro.[12] Although he wrote several of the most accomplished poems about the Black experience and social justice, pieces like "Middle Passage," "Runagate,

Runagate," "Frederick Douglass," and "Homage to the Empress of
the Blues," he would not embrace Black cultural nationalism. At
any rate, Hayden, who served on the conference planning committee, knew he would be facing a largely hostile audience—not
as a poet, he was warmly applauded at the literary reading—but
as a panelist. *Negro Digest* editor David Llorens captures his performance:

> Reading lines from Yeats, Hayden solemnly commented, "I
> don't have to be Irish to love those lines.
>   "Let's quit saying we're black writers writing to black
> folks—it has been given importance it should not have."
> Hayden's anticipation of opposition gave way to a slight
> stutter. "I don't think we're consciously trying to escape."
>   His sensibility shaken to the point of anger, Hayden
> continued: "Please notice this—all you folks sitting out
> there waiting to jump down my neck." He proceeded to define
> poetry as "the beauty of perception given form . . . the art of
> saying the impossible." (Llorens 62)

Hayden's proposal for a more nuanced understanding of any
writer's role and work failed to sway many in the crowd.

Tolson indeed proved dynamic. Although in his mid-sixties and
battling stomach cancer to which he would succumb only four
months later, he turned in a performance that Killens surely appreciated. As depicted by Llorens: "The audience, now spellbound,
listened as the man who might affectionately be called the grandfather of the conference spoke of the tridimensionality of man,
'A man has his biology, his sociology, and his psychology—*and
then he becomes a poet*'" (62). "Tolson then looked mischievously
at Hayden and bellowed, 'I'm a black poet, an African-American
poet, a Negro poet. I'm no accident—and I don't give a tinker's
damn what you think'" (63).

Tolson, a former dramatist and long-time debate coach, probably would have been too much of a match for Hayden rhetorically
even if the audience had been neutral. In front of the assemblage

in Jubilee Hall, incited by Killens, both before and at the conference (to be partial to Tolson's analysis), Hayden had no shot. Ironically, Hayden and Tolson were not that far apart aesthetically, often grouped together as examples of technically excellent Black modernists (which also drew Tolson, the more obscure of the two, some criticism from Black Aestheticians).[13] And there was considerable mutual respect between the two poets, who had known each other for years. In 1952 they both participated in the landmark Festival of Negro Poets at Jackson State College, and Tolson recalled how impressed he was with Hayden's ability to transfix the audience by reading "Homage to the Empress of the Blues."[14] Hayden included Tolson in the 1967 anthology *Kaleidoscope*, writing in the head notes, seemingly in appreciation, that in Tolson's poetry exists "the consciousness, expressed very often with ironic humor, of what it means to be a Negro in the Western World" (57). Obviously the crowd at Fisk was not choosing between the two based on an assessment of their writing.

In any event, Tolson's conception both echoed and prefigured words uttered by Killens. In the 1965 *Negro Digest* symposium, Killens wrote, "I am not just *any* American. I am a special kind of an American, known as the Negro, invented by America for the special purpose of exploitation. Therefore, I *am* different. I look at life from the vantage point (for better or worse) of being an American Negro" ("Task of the Negro Writer as Artist" 74). In his 1971 self-interview, "Rappin' with Myself," he asked, "[H]ow in the hell could I be a writer who happens to be Black? I wasn't born pecking on a typewriter" (103). He argued that every African American is born Black in a racist nation and that the crucial facts for African-American writers are their roots and Black cultural frame of reference. In his view, "a cat would have to be really out to lunch to give up all that just for the questionable distinction of being 'a writer who happens to be a colored man'" (103).

The theme of the 1967 conference, held April 21–23, was "The Black Writer and Human Rights." Along with Killens, the speakers were John Henrik Clarke, LeRoi Jones, Ron Milner, Ronald Fair, Lerone Bennett, Margaret Danner, and Gwendolyn Brooks.

The audience thus heard several speeches that continued the dominant, revolutionary tenor of the previous year's event, addresses that aligned with the general sensibility of the students, who made up most of the crowd, and the sentiments of the popular conference director. *Negro Digest* reported:

> The growth of Black consciousness on the Fisk campus was evident. It is not possible to gauge novelist John O. Killens' direct influence on this phenomenon, but the writer's relaxed, informal manner, and his total lack of pomp and preten[s]ion, cannot but have proved a remarkable change for a faculty member on the campus. The thrust of his relationship with the student has been to narrow the distance between teacher and student rather than to expand it. ("On the Conference Beat" 92)[15]

The most significant occurrence, a development that widely influenced discourses on African-American cultural politics, was the "rebirth" of Gwendolyn Brooks. Although the work of the celebrated poet had always reflected deep concern for and understanding of Black humanity, her artistic vision had been mostly connected, according to biographer George Kent, to the white liberal critical consensus. "Suddenly," as Brooks writes in her autobiography *Report from Part One,* "there was New Black to meet" (84).[16]

Although not youngsters, the historians Clarke and Bennett functioned as "New Blacks" who served to persuade Brooks about the virtues of Black Power and Black cultural nationalism. Clarke described enslavement as an assault on African identity and asserted that literature like the slave narratives was survival oriented. He then traced a movement from the slave narratives through a literature of restoration, as typified by the work of Du Bois, a literature of protest, as exemplified by the fiction of Richard Wright, to the advent of neo-slave narratives, as demonstrated by the writings of Killens, Baldwin, and Kelley. Clarke summed up by stating, "It is singularly the mission of the Black writer to tell his people what they have been in order for them to understand what they are. And from this the people will clearly understand what they must be" (qtd. in Kent 197). Bennett had argued in the 1965 *Negro Digest* symposium for a politically engaged art that would create new forms of expression and divorce itself from the "white culture structure" (78). He conveyed a similar message at Fisk, finding it astonishing that "a man or an oppressed person would choose to address his oppressors, primarily" (qtd. in Kent 198).

On her own subsequent panel, Brooks and fellow poet Margaret Danner were introduced somewhat rudely, a fact that perturbed Killens, by a student who suggested that no African-American poetry of relevance to the Black struggle had been published between the Harlem Renaissance and contemporary outpourings by Black cultural nationalists. Both Danner and Brooks, whose work had been done during the in-between period, took exception, but Danner, scheduled to speak first, was the one who reproached the student. Before her own presentation, which consisted mostly of reading poetry, Brooks issued a brief statement. Allowing that "race fed testimony" will find itself into Black art, she concluded, "I continue and violently to believe that, whatever the stimulating persuasion, poetry, not journalism, must be the result of involvement with emotions and ideas and ink and paper." Then she remarked, "And that's all the vital prose that I have for you, Mr. Killens" (qtd. in Kent 199).

Brooks's remarks were respectfully received as were her verses, which included selections like "Malcolm X," "Kitchenette Building," "The Mother," "We Real Cool," and "The Ballad of Rudolph Reed." She apologized for the fact that some of her poems treating the issue of social justice were too long to read. Concerning the response by the students, Kent notes that "although they would have to admit that Gwendolyn's poetry was a powerful element in the human rights struggle, their ultimate demand came closer to being satisfied by a literature that asserted a hearty rejection of middle-class values, a violent response to oppression, and an exclusive identification with the black community" (200). In other words, they were more interested in Ron Milner and the conference's biggest draw, LeRoi Jones. Near the end of Brooks's performance, Jones entered the hall and Brooks announced his arrival. Kent observes that "from that moment, the conference was in the hands of the more radical social critics and the visionary young" (200).

On the drama panel, Milner avowed, "If a new Black theater is to be born, sustain itself, and justify its own being, it must go home. Go home psychically, mentally, aesthetically, and I think physically" (qtd. in Kent 201). Jones's comments about theater complemented Milner's; then, at the audience's request, he turned into a performing poet, reading works like "A Poem for Half-White College Students." Given the rapturous response of the students, Kent concludes that "the Milner-Jones panel fully dramatized the marriage of the Black Power and Black Arts movements and the hard tones and desperation of life in the Northern ghettoes" (201–2).

Brooks's immersion into the environment of the conference—proud and angry students denouncing integration—caused her to reconsider her specific notions of art and its relationship to the African-American social and political struggle. She later wrote, "I didn't know what to make of what surrounded me, of what with hot sureness began almost immediately to invade me. I had never been before, in the general presence of such insouciance, such live firmness, such confident vigor, such determination to mold or carve something DEFINITE" (85). Back home in Chicago, she became active in working with young African-American writers. Some, like Don L. Lee, would become important in their own right. She supported Black cultural initiatives and, ultimately, severed her longstanding ties with Harper and Row. In 1969 she began publishing with Broadside Press, a Black independent publishing company in Detroit founded by poet Dudley Randall. She became perhaps the major African-American author who most put her manuscripts where her mouth was, and she has been seen as a model of commitment for numerous African-American writers and publishers.

The 1968 conference took place two weeks after the assassination of Martin Luther King, Jr. In his opening address, Killens urged the mostly student body to agitate for political and cultural change. A later version of his speech would be published as the essay "The Black Writer and the Revolution." The conference theme, "The Black Writer's Vision for America," harkened back to the New School affair (*Black* replacing *Negro* to reflect changing linguistic and cultural consciousness). Featured were Lee and such panelists as Charles V. Hamilton, Piri Thomas, and Sarah Webster Fabio. Julian Mayfield—novelist, essayist, playwright, and actor—delivered the keynote address.

In the context of Killens's "orchestration," the involvement of Mayfield is especially worth noting. Mayfield, an original member of the Harlem Writers Guild, had been abroad since 1961, residing in Ghana (a neighbor to Du Bois in the latter's final years) until 1966, and then in Europe and Asia until 1967. He was among the creative and literary artists criticized in the then newly published *Crisis of the Negro Intellectual*, and he was the first to issue a rebuttal. That statement was titled "Crisis or Crusade?" and appeared in the June 1968 issue of *Negro Digest*, which means that it is likely that the lengthy, fifteen-page review was both finished and the subject of some discussion between Mayfield and Killens prior to the Fisk gathering. However, Killens's letter of invitation to Mayfield dated January 10, 1968, is very brief and perfunctory, providing no sense that the two writers even knew each other on a personal level.[17] It is still possible, though, that the featuring of Mayfield, who defends Killens, can be viewed as an indirect response to Cruse.

Aside from dismissing Cruse's book as a dismal failure overall, despite its often brilliant economic analyses, Mayfield cites several of the expressions of petty jealousy, historical inaccuracies, and telling omissions that mark Cruse's work. For example, he attributes the harsh chapter on Lorraine Hansberry to the fact that Hansberry had refused to read the manuscript of a play Cruse had written. He accuses Cruse, justly so, of trying to pass himself off as a longtime Black nationalist while not revealing that he was a Marxist theoretician in the 1940s, a favored Black son of the organized left wing in Harlem, and had been ideologically in league with many people he later scorns. Mayfield clinches his argument by recounting an incident that occurred when he traveled to Cuba with a delegation that included Cruse in 1960, an episode during which Cruse reportedly, backed by two white women, berated a Cuban aide because food and drink were not readily available. Cruse is alleged to have exclaimed, "[Y]ou damn well better get us something to eat and drink or I'll go back to the States and write the worst things I can think of about you and your damned Revolution!" (23–24). Mayfield claims that he wrote those words down that night, words that in his view spoke to an essential vindictiveness that lay at the heart of Cruse's character, and checked them against the recollections of others before publishing the 1968 review. He then remarks that "the man who screamed that blackmail threat, merely for food and water, is the author of *The Crisis of the Negro Intellectual,* the political pundit who presumes to sit in moral judgment on almost every black person who has written and published a book, a play or a poem" (24).[18]

Another interesting twist to the 1968 conference, a case of planting literary seed that would bear fruit, was the appearance of Lee, who had been recommended by Gwendolyn Brooks and was attending his first Black Writers Conference. Both Lee, later Haki Madhubuti, of course, and Killens served as writers-in-residence at Howard University in the 1970s and worked together on several conferences there. Ultimately, it has been Madhubuti who has since 1991 been able to maintain the annual writers' conference for which Killens called.

Of the Howard University conferences held between 1974 and 1978, the first, held in November 1974, was the most significant. By the beginning of the 1970s, the ranks of African Americans who were optimistic about social and political revolution had apparently thinned, which is not hard to fathom. Much crucial Black leadership had been eliminated—whether they were far left exemplars like the Black Panthers, nationalist visionaries like Malcolm X, or mainstream direct actionists like King. Such events bred nihilism or a belief that an oppressive establishment will always prevail. To demonstrate that Black was Beautiful could be done rather quickly, but to demonstrate that Black was powerful enough to sustain Black beauty over the long haul was another matter. It seemed that the symbolic Black transformation of the 1960s was waning—fewer Afros, dashikis, tiki sticks, rallies, slogans. Killens himself had treated these affectations satirically in parts of *The Cotillion*. The post-riots, "Great Society" influx of money into the Black community was diminishing. Nixon was in the White House, Moynihan a chief advisor, and the age of "benign neglect" was underway. Thus the 1974 conference at Howard stands as the first major African-American writers' conference of a new political era.[19]

Killens directed this conference under the auspices of the Institute for the Arts and Humanities using the same theme as the 1966 conference at Fisk, only the title was changed, again to reflect new thinking, from "The Image of the Negro in American Literature" to "The Image of Black Folk in American Literature." The scale was larger than it had been at Fisk. Whereas there had been eight to ten panelists at the Fisk conferences, there were twenty-nine at Howard. Participants quite familiar to Killens like John Henrik Clarke, Ossie Davis, Maya Angelou, Alice Childress, Piri Thomas, Paule Marshall, Ron Milner, Mari Evans, and Haki Madhubuti were on hand as well as writers who had gained prominence since the Fisk conferences like Ishmael Reed, Quincy Troupe, Kalamu ya Salaam, and Richard Wesley.

In his expansive opening remarks that were titled the same as the conference theme, Killens urged fellow writers to unify in an effort to change the negative images that many Black people had of themselves, conceptions that were created and/or reinforced by media moguls on Madison Avenue and in Hollywood. He noted the recent proliferation of Blaxploitation movies like *Superfly* and the frequent use of the word "nigger" by Redd Foxx and Richard Pryor, informing the audience that in the words of Louis Reyes Rivera, "[T]here ain't no chinks in the People's Republic. There ain't no spicks in Cuba" ("The Image of Black Folk in American Literature" 49). The creation of the "nigger," to his way of thinking, was the work of oppressors who attempted to justify the inferior status of slaves to themselves, to the outside world, and to the enslaved populace. He also spoke of the role that writers like Mark Twain, William Faulkner, Margaret Mitchell, and Robert Penn Warren played in promoting stereotypes of Blacks. Even while acknowledging that Harriet Beecher Stowe's *Uncle Tom's Cabin* was a "powerful weapon against American slavery," Killens suggested that the novel made widespread a host of stereotypes like the "loyal slave," the "kindly master," the "mulatto slave whose rebelliousness is solely the product of his or her white blood," and the contrasting "naturally submissive pure African" (49–50). Killens pointed out that these stereotypes cannot account for Nat Turner, Denmark Vesey, Harriet Tubman, Ann Nzinga, Toussaint L' Ouverture, Gabriel Prosser, and Cinque. He stressed that if African-American writing were to be geared toward liberation, a rhetorical purpose he felt was proper, then constructing images that contributed to "debrainwashing," to "deniggerizing," had to be a primary activity for African-American writers. Speaking more broadly, he proposed that African-American writers create a new vision, perhaps socialist or Pan-Africanist, that privileges people over things. And speaking organizationally, he suggested the formation of a national Black Writers Congress to "deal with the special and mutual problems faced by all Black writers, literarily, politically and economically" (51). Attempting to move beyond largely symbolic gestures or what he termed the "rap-style rhetoric" of the 1960s, he offered the offices of the institute as a means to found such an entity (45, 51).

Killens, again reflecting on what he regarded as weaknesses evident in the previous decade, wove a feminist strand into his speech. He argued for women's equality in the Black Liberation Movement, reminding the audience that "no revolution has made it in this Twentieth Century without the liberation of their woman being one of the top priorities" (47). He posited (and read from them) that the two most revolutionary poems of the previous forty years were written by Black women, Margaret Walker's "For

My People" and Mari Evans's "Speak the Truth to the People" (51–52).

According to Carole A. Parks, there was a supportive consensus among the participants regarding Killens's perspective on the hazards of negative images and the exigence to create positive ones. As playwright-critic Eugene Perkins remarked, "[I]mage-making should be a part of Black theater because from images we get models, from models, direction" (qtd. in Parks, "National Black Writers Convention" 88). But the group also expressed concerns, even disagreement, about how to disperse the magnificent images generated. Ossie Davis, delivering the keynote address, declared that technical expertise, access to mechanisms of production, and a broad yet sharply focused political outlook were necessary for all the proposed creation of positive images to have maximum impact. As he reasoned, "[S]eldom do we show our images connected with *power*. There is time for continuing to show how clever, how beautiful and talented we are. But we must have an international perspective on power" (qtd. in "National Black Writers Convention" 88). Despite exhortations like Davis's and the fact that 250–600 people jammed the meeting sessions, less than 100 showed up to discuss the most concrete organizational proposal made at the conference, the formation of a Black Writers Congress. Undoubtedly, some were wary about which artistic tastes and policies would be dominant in such a group. Nonetheless, Ron Milner's comments rang ironically. Defending certain achievements of the 1960s, Milner argued that "rhetoric was tested right in the middle of rhetoric. The fire burned off the fat, left the lean, so we knew what and who was real" (qtd. in "National Black Writers Convention" 90). To Killens's dismay, apparently real was the lack of a strong enough collective will to establish a Black writers' association.

Even in the 1980s, Killens took every opportunity he could to push the idea that African-American writers should place their creative energies in the service of Black liberation efforts. However, his particular message may not have been reaching many

ears by then. To be sure, there was still considerable talk about
positive and negative images in the African-American community, but much of it had splintered along gender lines. The 1970s
and 1980s had seen the spectacular rise and commercial success of
Black female writers. Some of the more popular, Ntozake Shange
and Alice Walker in particular, were often accused of "bashing"
Black men. Many women, in turn, claimed that Black men, particularly writers, who as a whole had not painted flattering portray-
als of Black women, were simply jealous. Shange's controversial
choreopoem, *for colored girls who have considered suicide/when the
rainbow is enuf*, was staged on Broadway in 1976, won an Obie
Award, and was nominated for a Tony, an Emmy, and a Grammy.
In 1983, Alice Walker received the Pulitzer Prize for *The Color
Purple*. Killens, fully aware of those developments, made critical remarks about both *colored girls* and Walker's novel, although
those comments were more tempered than those he made in 1952
about Ellison's *Invisible Man*. He spoke about the absence of "hero
dynamics" in *colored girls*. And while acknowledging that he considered Walker a fine writer craftwise, he added that he sometimes
had problems with her content. As was the case with the Ellison
article, he proved to be a somewhat stern reviewer in his search
for positive literary role models.[20]

By the mid-1980s, Killens, then writer-in-residence at Medgar
Evers College in Brooklyn, was angling toward directing yet another conference. This one would be held March 21–23, 1986,
and titled "The Social Responsibilty of the Writer to the Community." The topic was certainly timely once again given the intense
discussions about stereotypes underway in African-American literary circles. However, after the film release of *The Color Purple*
near the end of 1985, the issue of negative and positive images
became the hottest cultural topic in virtually all quarters of the
Black community. This partly explains why more than two thousand registrants turned out for what became the largest event that
Killens directed. Another key factor was that many folks turned
out in tribute to a man, now seventy years old, who still was working tirelessly to promote literature as a tool for radically demo-

cratic social change. On hand were thirty invited speakers, including many who by then had longstanding ties to Killens or had participated in one or more of the previous conferences, writers such as Margaret Walker, Maya Angelou, Toni Cade Bambara, Ishmael Reed, Calvin Hernton, Phil Petrie, Samuel Yette, Sonia Sanchez, Quincy Troupe, Amiri Baraka, Lonne Elder III, Richard Wesley, Addison Gayle, and Mari Evans. In fact, it was Evans, just as she had informed Killens's comments at the 1974 Howard conference, who provided the impetus for the conference director's greetings that were printed in the program: "During the glorious and turbulent Sixties, our poet Mari Evans called upon us to SPEAK THE TRUTH TO THE PEOPLE. Yet, to follow her counsel today may very well be to risk banishment from the publishing establishment. Faced with this harsh reality, the question of the writer's 'Social Responsibility' becomes crucial to our cultural survival" (3).

In his welcoming remarks at the conference on the morning of March 22, Killens began by telling the audience that writers, educators, and communicators have a responsibility to remain angry, though not despairing, about racism in the country. As mentioned earlier, he spoke, as Baldwin had at the 1965 New School conference, of the need to get America to face up to its history. Again he railed against negative depictions of African Americans in the mass media. Then, for maybe the final time in the public gaze, certainly the final time before an audience that large, he turned forcefully to his favorite topic, one that had consumed so much of his life's energy and creative effort. Using his own previous books as sources for anecdotes, he spoke, naturally, of the centrality of Black literary heroes to social struggle:

> We are a great people. But where are the novels, the dramas,
> the epics about Saint Harriet of the Eastern Shore? Saint
> Medgar and Saint Fannie Lou of 'Sippi? Saint Rosa of
> Montgomery? Saint Malcolm of Nebraska? Saint Martin
> of Atlanta? The great Saint Paul of Rutgers? Where are the
> epics? Where are the monuments to their greatness? We need

more literature and celebration of our nobility as a people. However, some of our writers are too busy getting over with the people that despise us, which means that fundamentally some of us despise ourselves. Too many of us are afraid to rock the boat. . . .

Our purpose must be to capsize that sucker, if necessary, and construct a boat which will, in the immortal words of Margaret Walker, "accommodate all the faces/all the Adams and Eves and their countless generations." Black writers must be boat rockers. Rock the boat. Capsize it. Drown the racist occupants.

Sisters and brothers, the Black writer, educator, and communicator are in an all out war for the minds of our own people, especially with the corporate media. It is total war sisters and brothers. And in this cultural revolution, we must wage guerilla warfare, even as this country did in the revolution against the British, even as the valiant guerilla fighters did in Vietnam against the greatest amassment of power the world has ever known, the armed might of the U.S.A. Even as our oppressors have used the English language as a weapon to degrade us, we must use the language to our own purposes. Metaphorically speaking, we must ambush the bastards, capture their weapons—the Anglo-Saxon language—and beat the hell out of them with their own weaponry. As my comrades used to say in the Army during World War II, "kicking asses and taking names." And in my humble opinion, that is precisely what the Black writer must be about. Excuse me. Take note. I said "kicking," not "kissing," "k-i-c-k," not "k-i-s-s." Life can be so confusing if you prefer to be confused.[21]

At that evening's dinner in his honor, Killens thanked all in attendance for their support and allowed that such support encouraged him in his efforts. Although he was visibly tired, even seriously ill, he read from Langston Hughes's poem "Mother to Son" and announced that he fully intended to "keep on keeping on." He asserted that the powers that be, chief among them the media and the board of education, were in a countercultural revolution. And as he had done at previous conferences dating back to 1959, he called for a permanent National Black Writers Conference, adding to that call a reiteration of the writers' union idea and the question of forming an "amalgamated Black press" to ensure that Black myths, legends, plays, and films are disseminated. He closed by reading from the greetings in the conference booklet: "We can take this beachhead and maintain it, if we work tirelessly, and fearlessly. We must push forward, for there is nought behind us save the open sea. The open sea and vicious sharks. And Moby Dick" (3).

As to be expected, much of the Killens viewpoint was amplified at the conference by Margaret Walker, Maya Angelou, Toni Cade Bambara, Mari Evans, Sonia Sanchez, Amiri Baraka, Addison Gayle, and Samuel Yette. They all urged in some way the Black writer or cultural worker to show a commitment to the Black community. For example, Margaret Walker, herself seventy years old and introduced by Killens as the "Empress of the Black Experience," noted that "Black writers are tied to the Black world and are responsible to it." However, Walker's nationalism, like Killens's, opened onto a broader outlook as she forecast a "new people's socialism of the twenty-first century" and a "pluralistic people's world." She urged African-American writers to "behold the vision and begin the task."

Maya Angelou spoke of a double responsibility: individual concern for one's artistic development and collective concern for the advancement of Black people. Making veiled references to the controversy surrounding *The Color Purple*, she stressed the need for African Americans to exhibit love toward one another if they aim to progress as a group. And she noted that the theme of love has always been a central although perhaps overlooked quality of African-American poetry.

Toni Cade Bambara and Mari Evans directly addressed the disputes over *The Color Purple*. Bambara, who saw the responsibility of the Black writer to be that of reminding people of what they are pretending not to know, denounced the round of *"Purple* debates" as largely a diversion promoted by elements of the media to di- minish efforts to dismantle apartheid in South Africa or mobilize protest around the MOVE bombing in Philadelphia.

Evans argued that "our first responsibility to the community is to be at peace with our African selves, with that matrix, with who we really are before we're Republican, Democrat, hippie, flower child, feminist, gay, lesbian, universal, whatever. If we're clear about that, we can be clear about everything else." She offered that "the real issue is not Alice Walker." Evans suggested that those in attendance focus on what they could, in fact, control, things like the building of a Black cultural infrastructure and being proactive with respect to issues like the disproportionately high incarceration rate of Black people and the proper care of Black children. Evans added that the African-American artist draws from the group, thus owes the group, and she cited Du Bois's "Cri- teria of Negro Art" (Killens could think of no better reference) as a rationale for self-consciously political literary works.

Sonia Sanchez, in one of the most moving presentations at the conference, exhorted artists and others to form a broad progres- sive alliance to combat racism and economic exploitation. She mentioned the Middle Passage, the genocide of Native Ameri- cans, South African apartheid, the expanding prison-industrial complex in the United States, the invasion of Grenada, the dan- ger posed by nuclear waste, the MOVE bombing, and the Atlanta child murders as political developments to which there had been inadequate responses. Asserting that "Americonomics" (her syn- onym for the economic policies of the Reagan administration) was a systematic attack on people to discourage activism, she called for the "building of institutions and consciousness not tied to the swing of capital." Also alluding, somewhat obliquely, to the *Purple* brouhaha, Sanchez admonished, "If you are doing, you don't have time to talk about other writers."

Amiri Baraka contended that the crucial issue with respect to literary assessment is the political allegiance of the artist and that all artists have an objective relationship to society despite whatever subjective pronouncements they may make. He rejected pure formalism as "complete freak out and denial of responsibility" and added that the African-American artistic movement always proceeded hand-in-hand with social struggle. The primary responsibility of the artist, Baraka espoused, is to "reflect the community at its most conscious," to compose work that is democratic and revolutionary.

Addison Gayle, always among the most sympathetic of literary critics when it came to Killens, sounded much like him as he declared, on the screenwriting panel, that "we need movies, good ones, about Malcolm X, Martin Luther King, Jr., and Sojourner Truth." Gayle added that as a writer, "you're always responsible to somebody."

Samuel Yette, from whom, in fact, Killens borrowed the term "hero dynamics," warned that the media were dangerously monopolized and too closely aligned with the government, with the result being that "a true adversarial relationship is lost, so is freedom of the press, and so is freedom."[22] As expected, he also pointed to the media's role in "devaluing Blacks and other people of color and fostering self-hate and other destructive behavior patterns." To Yette, Black journalists should "view their time in white media as tentative" and work toward owning their own outlets.

The 1986 conference proved to be the last formal set of affirmations and testimonials that Killens would hear in person, the final punctuation mark of his "public text." The voices he called on and merged with over the course of several decades helped him place before thousands the cultural initiatives he outlined in 1959. More efforts than we can yet tally with regard to literary output, publishing, and cultural organizing have been spawned by his continual need to discuss collective improvement and his willingness to assemble the folks.

conclusion

In her 1971 essay "Tripping with Black Writing," Sarah Webster Fabio identifies a group of daring writers whom she labels "escapees from the prisons of Anglo rhetoric" and "frontiersman in the lumbering netherlands of Black language" (228). She lists each member of the group and adds succinct phrases about his or her achievement and influence.[1] About John Oliver Killens, one of the escapees, she writes, "Killens. Killens' chilluns. On their jobs. Taking care of business. 'Deniggerizing the world'" (228). If this is now understood to be Killens's essential impact as a writer, that is, creating and inspiring Black vernacular art that promotes positive images of African Americans, he would find that a fairly acceptable outcome. He certainly sought, especially through his fiction, to ennoble people of African descent and to celebrate their culture.[2] As indicated, that mission led him to settle for characters that, with their Du Boisian uprightness, are somewhat thin psychologically. In fact, Robby Youngblood, Solly Saunders (an exception to the rule), Chuck Othello, and Killens's Pushkin, at a minimum, can be considered one serial character. However, the fictional whole in this case is greater than the sum of its parts. The uncompromising central intelligence at the heart of the Killens oeuvre, one that moves beyond glorifying to keep the volume pumped up about anti-Black racism and white supremacist brainwashing, is a precious entity in African-American literature. That such wisdom is encoded artistically in Black verbal forms, especially African-American humor, and has served as a model for younger writers stands as one of Killens's major rhetorical accomplishments. Fabio was also alluding, I imagine, to a political platform endorsed by the writer, one that stressed Black unity,

Black commitment, Black self-determination, Black resistance, and Black self-defense.

Included in Killens's attempt to change or deniggerize the world was a continual verbal assault on literary, media, and educational establishments relative to their collectively abysmal record of promoting positive Black images. This question of portrayal was central to the many literary gatherings he spearheaded, although the issue hardly represented a new concern in the wider discourse on cultural politics. As far back as 1926, the same year Du Bois published "Criteria of Negro Art," *The Crisis* was already reporting on the "long controversy" about how Blacks should be depicted by writers and visual artists ("Questionnaire" 165). A questionnaire containing seven items concerning the obligation of writers and publishers appeared in the February 1926 issue.[3] Responses, including those by Carl Van Vechten, H. L. Mencken, Langston Hughes, Walter White, Alfred Knopf, Jessie Fauset, Georgia Douglas Johnson, and Charles Chesnutt, were featured in subsequent issues throughout the year. Although some conference participants undoubtedly found it irksome to have to revisit such a troublesome topic again and again, Killens remained passionate about the matter and steadfastly assembled voices around him to call for a mostly heroic treatment of African-American characters.

Beyond the dimension of Black nationalism, we can perceive other aspects of the Killens project, political and economic elements that were never totally submerged. Surely, Killens would speak passionately about the revolutionary possibilities of Black art in terms of the Black liberation movement, pressing the fact that "I write in a Black idiom to be dug by Black folks in the first instance" ("Rappin' with Myself" 103). But he would just as frequently add, sometimes immediately, that he also composes "for all people in the second" (103–4). Concern with the secondary audience, the "all people," marked his work with a broad, even socialist, humanism, which is especially evident in the jeremiad *Black Man's Burden*, a book that notably informed the political and economic positions taken by Stokely Carmichael and Charles V. Hamilton in *Black Power: The Politics of Liberation in*

America (see 38–41). After Killens warns the nation against valuing free enterprise rather than free people, he advises, "We in America need to reconstruct our society so that people take precedence over property, and all men—white, black, brown, yellow—are masters, and only things are slaves" (166–67). He could otherwise envision no humane, truly prosperous, or stable nation, or entire world for that matter, as suggested by the utopian conclusion of *And Then We Heard the Thunder.* Ironically, in October 1987, as Killens lay upon his deathbed, the Dow Jones Industrial Average plunged 508 points in one day, sending financial markets into panic. Was it eerie affirmation of his views?

Killens was an artist very secure among Black people, Black fellow artists and activists in particular. In a 1984 interview he pointed out, "The writer has to reconcile the very serious contradictions: the absolute need for solitude to do his or her work and the absolute need for experiences with other people" (Peeples, "Artist as Liberator" 14). He offered further, "It would seem to me the writer should be a writer/activist. The writer should involve himself or herself wherever his or her people are struggling so that he or she can understand the meaning of struggle and interpret the struggle in his or her work" (14). It appears that the string of writers' conferences Killens organized also functioned as partial attempts to bridge realities that some, although not the majority of the panelists he would invite, would consider forever to be mutually exclusive. He put in his long and isolated hours at the typewriter, but as a naturally gregarious person he had an insatiable need, despite the great demand on his time, to convene events that drew others around him for discussions and presentations about literature and politics. The conferences he directed between 1965 and 1986 (he had begun planning another for 1988) stand alongside his writing as important milestones in African-American literary history.

A compulsive storyteller even away from the typewriter, Killens left behind a series of rich oral narratives. Some we're still trying to figure out. He related one about the discipline involved in cutting two hundred pages, at the publisher's request, from the manuscript that became *Youngblood,* which originally ran more than one thousand pages; another about that trimmed text turning up in *'Sippi* and other pieces. He told how a branch of the military purchased (or at least he heard so) thousands of copies of *And Then We Heard the Thunder* to dump into the ocean. One more about looking out from a hotel room in Tashkent in the Soviet Union, a place he had heard about from Langston Hughes, and watching native Blacks slap each other five in greeting. This was a favorite as it spoke to a worldwide brotherhood and sisterhood of Blackness that was in line with his vision.[4]

Intending to convey political messages with his stories, Killens was in league, in this regard, with Hughes, Richard Wright, Margaret Walker, and, of course, Du Bois. "All art is propaganda," he would agree with Du Bois, then counsel, but "all propaganda is not art" ("Rappin' with Myself" 135).

Last but not least, he was truly his great-grandmother's literary and rhetorical heir. As they sat around the fireplace or walked the streets of his childhood Macon together, she would spin tales of the nobility of her people and inform young John, "Aaah, Lord, Honey, THE HALF AIN'T NEVER BEEN TOLD," thereby directing him toward his life's work ("The Half Ain't Never Been Told" 279). Killens later reflected, remembering images of his great-grandmother, "I could see her cocoa-colored face deepened with reddish-purple tones of African sunsets, hear her voice and it became a challenge to me to one day to try to tell that half that had not been told. It was the half that I would tell part of, at the very least. I felt I owed that much to Granny" (279). He kept alive the flame of her African-American pride all the way to the end.

John Oliver Killens was a great storyteller—and story.

notes

.

INTRODUCTION

1. The Harlem Writers Guild was founded in 1950. Original members included Rosa Guy, John Henrik Clarke, and Walter Christmas. Members and alumni of the guild—such as Maya Angelou, Ossie Davis, Paule Marshall, Terry McMillan, and Walter Dean Myers—have produced hundreds of book-length or feature-length works of fiction, nonfiction, poetry, drama, and film. The Pulitzer Prize nominations were for the 1962 novel *And Then We Heard the Thunder* and the 1971 novel *The Cotillion*. Addison Gayle dubbed Killens the "spiritual father of the new novelists" in *The Way of the New World*, 261. Surprisingly, however, Gayle omits serious discussion of Killens's 1967 novel, '*Sippi*, from his analysis.

2. See Gayle, *The Way of the New World*, 261–77; and Bell, *The Afro-American Novel and Its Tradition*, 247–52.

3. See Neal, "And Shine Swam On"; and Neal, "The Black Arts Movement."

4. This definition of *rhetoric* is admittedly reductive. However, no consensus definition has emerged; the purpose of the one I offer is to focus attention on certain aspects of Killens's prose.

5. See Rampersad, *The Life of Langston Hughes*, 221–23.

CHAPTER 1

1. In "The Ethics of Living Jim Crow" Wright describes how he was beaten by his mother for participating in a fight with white boys. Although he had gotten the worst of the battle, he was punished because his mother wanted him to learn deference toward whites in order to improve his chances of survival in the South.

2. Killens, for example, titled an essay "Downsouth-Upsouth." See *Black Man's Burden*, 55–96. He subsequently references that essay in his introduction to *Black Southern Voices*, 2–3.

3. This excerpt is from a speech delivered by Douglass, "The Significance of Emancipation in the West Indies," 204.

4. Du Bois's 1903 essay "The Talented Tenth" and the 1948 essay, "The Talented Tenth Memorial Address," are reprinted back-to-back in Henry Louis Gates, Jr., and Cornel West's *Future of the Race*, 133–77. In the latter essay Du Bois writes:

> Karl Marx stressed the fact that not merely the upper class but the mass of men were the real people of the world. He insisted that the masses were poor, ignorant, and sick, not by sin or by nature but by oppression. He preached that planned production of goods and just distribution of income would abolish poverty, ignorance and disease, and make the so-called upper-class, not the exception, but the rule among mankind. He declared that the world was not for the few, but for the many; that out of the masses of men could come overwhelming floods of ability and genius, if we freed men by plan and not by rare chance. Civilization not only could be shared by the vast majority of men, but such civilization founded on a wide human base would be better and more enduring than anything that the world has seen. The world would thus escape the enduring danger of being run by a selfish few for their own advantage.
>
> Very gradually as the philosophy of Karl Marx and many of his successors seeped into my understanding, I tried to apply this doctrine with regard to Negroes. My Talented Tenth must be more than talented, and work not simply as individuals. Its passport to leadership was not alone learning, but expert knowledge of modern economics as it affected American Negroes; and in addition to this and fundamental, would be its willingness to sacrifice and plan for such economic revolution in industry and just distribution of wealth, as would make the rise of our group possible. (162–63)

5. Killens wrote about his reverence for Du Bois, whom he termed Big Grand Daddy, on several occasions, including in "Rappin' with Myself," a self-interview. He speaks of Du Bois as Big Grand Daddy on pp. 114–15 and observes, "I was too much in respectful awe of this man Du Bois to call him my personal friend. You, a part of the great unwashed, do not call yourself a personal friend of the Patriarch, no matter how much you revere him. And that's the image he evoked for me. He was a beautifully arrogant aristocrat with a biting sense of irony and humor, and affected no false modesty. He had an objective evaluation of his importance and was not about to let you waste his time in discussion of the weather" (115). Also see Killens, introduction to *An ABC of Color*, 9.

6. In response to criticism from clergymen in Alabama, King's comments were made to justify his activism in sites beyond Atlanta and beyond the current legal system.

7. The "Sorrow Songs" is Du Bois's term for the spirituals in *The Souls of Black Folk*, 204–16.

8. For further views on the liberatory aspects of the spirituals, see Cone, *The Spirituals and the Blues*, 9–19; and Newman's introduction to *Go Down, Moses*, 23–24.

9. On page 93 of *The Cotillion*, Killens describes Lumumba's book collection as including works from "Du Bois, Baldwin, Spengler, Jones, Marx, Engels, Malcolm, Freud, Franklin, Bennett, Giovanni, Frazier, Hare, Douglass, Fair, Mitchell, Randall, Wright, Fanon, Hamilton, Ellison, Williams, Killens."

10. Killens made this comment to me during a series of conversations that took place between 1984 and 1986.

11. I was among a group of guests in 1986 to whom Killens proudly pointed out the Robeson poster.

12. Killens repeated these remarks on March 22, 1986, at the National Black Writers Conference at Medgar Evers College of the City University of New York.

13. This is one of several instances where Killens alludes to the comments made by Faulkner in the March 4, 1956 edition of the London *Sunday Times* that he would "fight for Mississippi against the United States, even if it meant going out into the street and shooting Negroes" (7) and to remarks made in a "A Letter to the North" that suggested that many Negroes in the South agreed with his views on gradualism and Northern agitators.

14. Black modes of discourse encompass, according to Smitherman, (1) call-and-response (Smitherman uses "call-response"), a series of spontaneous interactions between speaker and listener; (2) signification, the art of humorous put-downs, usually through verbal indirection; (3) tonal semantics, the conveying of meanings in Black discourse through specific kinds of voice rhythms and vocal inflections; and (4) narrative sequencing, the use of stories to explain and/or persuade. See *Talkin and Testifyin*, 101–66.

15. Ruth Finnegan observes that in *parallel phrasing*, "Each episode is related as a unit, and this full repetition of nearly similar events is one among the several means by which a skillful story-teller effectively heightens the tension and climax in his narration." See *Limba Stories and Story-Telling*, 79. She specifically defines *parataxis* as a construction where "sentences follow on one after the other as parallel formations complete in themselves rather than making up long periods of complex subordinate clauses" (75).

16. Concerning African-American ballads, N. I. White remarks, "There is hardly any such thing as a stanza belonging particularly to one song and to that alone. Generally speaking, practically any stanza is at home in practically any song." Qtd. in Gerould, *The Ballad of Traditon*, 268. LeRoi Jones comments in *Blues People* about how "certain technique and verses came to be standardized

among blues singers" (67). With respect to hip-hop, a more recent genre, borrowed phrases include "you jes tall, that's all," and some version of "we ain't
stoppin til 6 (sometimes 8) in the mornin." A more lengthy example of borrowing is Jay-Z's "I Just Wanna Love U (Give It to Me)." The following lines
are taken almost verbatim from his close associate The Notorious B.I.G.'s "The
World Is Filled": "When the Remi's in the system, ain't no tellin'/When I fuck
'em, will I diss 'em/That's what they be yellin':/I'm a pimp by blood, not rela-
tion/y'all be chasin', I replaced 'em, huh?/Drunk off Crys." Biggie's version goes:
"When the Remi's in the system, ain't no tellin/Will I fuck em will I diss em,
that's what these hoes yellin/I'm a pimp by blood, not relation/Y'all still chase
on, I'll replace on, punks/Drunk off Dom, silk and gators." Further linking the
borrowing in hip-hop to older musical forms and expanding the concept, scholar
Marcyliena Morgan notes in "Nuthin' But a G Thang":

> The recognition of influences—*giving props, representin', recognizin'*—
> as well as exposing artists who do not acknowledge the source of their
> materials, is accomplished by directly stating the name of a person or
> group during a rap and/or using the words or phrases of another artist
> who belong to the same crew. This often includes the use of simile
> and metaphor, which requires "local" Hip Hop knowledge in order
> to be understood. Local knowledge includes lived experiences as well
> as familiarity with popular culture. For instance, the use of the word
> "CREAM" indicates both respect for the group who popularized the
> term (the Wu-Tang Clan) and its meaning (Cash Rules Everything
> Around Me). (194)

17. Song of Solomon 1:5.
18. There are numerous versions of this tale, one of which is included under
the title "One Negro on Rye, Please!" in Spalding, *Encyclopedia of Black Folklore
and Humor,* 488.
19. Gayle, *The Way of the New World,* 261.
20. Novels in question include Williams, *The Man Who Cried I Am* and
Captain Blackman; Gaines, *Of Love and Dust* and *The Autobiography of Miss Jane
Pittman;* and Kelley, *A Different Drummer* and *Dunsfords Travels Everywhere.*
21. In "Rappin' with Myself," Killens speaks of Hughes's Pan-Africanism and
love of Black people. He also addresses the impact on him of Margaret Walker's
memorable poem "For My People" (101–3).

CHAPTER 2

1. Du Bois opens "The Talented Tenth" with the statement, "The Negro
race, like all races, is going to be saved by its exceptional men." He closes with

the almost identical statement, "The Negro race, like all other races, is going to be saved by its exceptional men" (133, 157).

2. About double consciousness Du Bois wrote, "It is a peculiar sensation, this double-consciousness, this sense of always looking at one's self through the eyes of others, of measuring one's soul by the tape of a world that looks on in amused contempt and pity. One ever feels his twoness,—an American, a Negro; two souls, two thoughts, two unreconciled strivings; two warring ideals in one dark body, whose dogged strength alone keeps it from being torn asunder" (*The Souls of Black Folk*, 5).

3. In a conversation with me on December 31, 1999, Grace Killens took issue with Vincent and maintained that *Youngblood* was destined all along to be her husband's first novel. She recalls papers being shipped home during the war with the title "Stony the Road We Trod," which was indeed the working title of the manuscript that became *Youngblood*. Killens himself, however, stated in a 1978 *Black Forum* interview with Revish Windham (5–6) that the work he sent home to his wife was about his war experiences. He said he decided to explore his childhood experiences in his first novel because the material about the war was too close to him for him to interpret it then.

4. In contrast, the "inside" method begins with identification and analysis of broad social contradictions within the system and then moves outward to consider character in relation to such social forces (Bell, *The Afro-American Novel and Its Tradition*, 247). Bell draws from Lukács, *Realism in Our Time*.

5. Langston Hughes opens the chapter "Harriet Tubman: The Moses of Her People" with this quote (35) in his *Famous American Negroes*, which he presented to the Killens children. See Killens, *Black Man's Burden*, 36.

6. In personal correspondence to me dated February 19, 1998, Deborah Breen wrote: "The Bainbridge story is based on the Brisbane riots, but there were also similar events in other cities, including Townsville and Cairns. . . . Killens may have chosen the name Bainbridge because similar riots occurred in England around the same time, near a town called Bainbridge. The basis of all these riots (as far as I know) was conflict between black American soldiers and white American soldiers, or conflict over enforced segregation." Breen also wrote: "It is very unlikely that John Oliver Killens was in Australia at the time of the riots, and his wife Grace Killens says it is more likely that he heard about the story from other soldiers he met after the incident. Coverage of the riots was censored in both the US and Australia at the time, but I have seen a couple of veiled references in letters from African American soldiers stationed in Australia who were writing back to newspapers in Baltimore and Chicago."

7. Often attributed to Solomon, in addition to Song of Solomon, are Proverbs, Ecclesiastes, and Psalms 72 and 127.

8. The idea of the crossroads or reckoning point is a recurrent theme in African-American culture exemplified by Robert Johnson's "Crossroads Blues": "I went to the crossroad, fell down on my knee,/Went to the crossroad, fell down

on my knee,/Asked the Lord above to have mercy, save poor Bob if you please."
See Hill, *Call & Response*, 802–3. Also note the ending, once again, of *12 Million
Black Voices* and the town Crossroads, Georgia, in *Youngblood*.

9. The "call me Mister" phrase is taken from the title of a section in Spalding,
Encyclopedia of Black Folklore and Humor, 446–60.

10. In Smitherman, *Black Talk*, 47, Amen Corner is defined as: "1) In the
Traditional Black Church (TBC), originally the place where the older members sit, especially older women, the Church 'mothers,' who are perceived as
the 'watchdogs of Christ' and who often lead the congregation in responsive
Amens. 2) Any section of the Church where the congregation uses many verbal
responses and *Amens*. 3) By extension, outside the Church world, a reference
to any area where there are expressions of strong support and high feeling for a
speaker or performer."

CHAPTER 3

1. A second founding charter, dated February 15, 1965, was not released
before Malcolm's assassination. The reason for the second "founding" was
doubtlessly connected to the OAAU's slow start. No more than a couple of
hundred people joined, and financial support proved meager. Malcolm, because
he embarked on a second and longer trip to Africa in 1964, had little time for
hands-on involvement in the organization's development.

2. For detailed discussion of Malcolm X's 1964 politics, see Breitman, *The
Last Year of Malcolm X*, 26–69, 141–52. Dyson's full discussion is in *Making
Malcolm*, "X Marks the Plots: A Critical Reading of Malcolm's Readers," 21–76.

3. In 1962 Ossie Davis invited Malcolm X to his home in Mount Vernon
to meet John Oliver Killens and others; Peter Bailey recalls that Killens was
in Harlem at the first planning meeting, in December 1963 or January 1964,
of what would become the OAAU. See Hampton and Fayer, *Voices of Freedom*,
250–52, 256–57. Taylor Branch reports a 1964 meeting between Clarence Jones,
the New York attorney for Martin Luther King, Jr., and Malcolm X that took
place at Sidney Poitier's home. Malcolm was escorted there by Killens. See *Pillar
of Fire*, 345.

4. In "The Half Ain't Never Been Told," Killens reflects on Malcolm. "All
of us loved Malcolm. He had been at our home where we now lived on Union
Street. We were home owners by now. Malcolm was a shy man with a tough and
tender strength. A very sensitive human being. We had been valued friends.
I had helped him put together the Organization for Afro-American Unity.
Philosophically speaking, Du Bois was my grandfather, Robeson was my father,
Malcolm was my brother" (296). In "Rappin' with Myself," he writes:

I loved Malcolm because he loved Black people and because he was
the antithesis of Gunga Din. He had a Black sense of humor that
would crack you up with laughter. He was an artist of the spoken word.
And like all true artists he was self-critical. He was getting Black folk
ready for the moment, for the national and international revolutionary
moment, so the establishment figured he had to go. Brother Malcolm's
mission was to deniggerize the earth. To rid the world of niggers. And
so like David Woodson said in 'Sippi, the establishment took notice of
him like the Romans did Jesus, and they said to themselves, "There's
a man teaching niggers to love themselves, teaching them that they
ain't niggers. He's a dangerous man. He'll mess up our whole damn
game if we ain't careful. We must get rid of him. We must get some
niggers to do him in." (118–19)

5. In a phone interview with Yusuf Nuruddin in 1998, Clarke suggested that
the help he and Killens gave Malcolm was more technical than substantive.

6. Killens visited Du Bois's home in Brooklyn Heights and had several occasions to visit and talk with King in Alabama. Killens alludes to these activities
in "Rappin' with Myself," 115, 119–20. Ralph Abernathy recounts in his autobiography that Killens was on the bill for the performance to be given at the
conclusion of the famous Selma-to-Montgomery March in 1965. See And the
Walls Came Tumbling Down, 355. For evidence of correspondence and meetings
between King and Killens, see Carson, The Papers of Martin Luther King, Jr.,
3:314–15, 4:46, 345, 605.

7. "Winter patriots" derives from Thomas Paine's American Crisis, originally
published in 1776. Paine asserted, "The summer soldier and the sunshine patriot
will, in this crisis, shrink from the service of their country; but he that stands
it now, deserves the love and thanks of man and woman" (890). In 1965,
Killens and Loften Mitchell coauthored a play titled Ballad of the Winter Soldier.
Mitchell attributes the title to Paine. See Peterson, "John Oliver Killens,"
293.

8. King wrote, in one of his characteristic statements about nonviolence,

The ultimate weakness of violence is that it is a descending spiral,
begetting the very thing it seeks to destroy. Instead of diminishing evil,
it multiplies it. Through violence you may murder the liar, but you
cannot murder the lie, nor establish the truth. Through violence you
may murder the hater, but you do not murder hate. In fact, violence
merely increases hate. So it goes. Returning violence for violence
multiplies violence, adding deeper darkness to a night already devoid
of stars. Darkness cannot drive out darkness: only light can do that.
Hate cannot drive out hate: only love can do that.

The beauty of nonviolence is that in its own way and its own time it seeks to break the chain reaction of evil. With a majestic sense of spiritual power, it seeks to elevate truth, beauty and goodness to the throne. Therefore I will continue to follow this method because I think it is the most practically sound and morally excellent way for the Negro to achieve freedom." (*Where Do We Go from Here*, 62–63)

9. The stanza from "Gunga Din" reads:

With 'is mussick on 'is back,
'E would skip with our attack,
An' watch us till the bugles made "Retire,"
An' for all 'is dirty 'ide
'E was white, clear white, inside
When 'e went to tend the wounded under fire! (Kipling, *Rudyard Kipling*, 328)

Gunga Din, in movie form, was released in 1939. William Faulkner contributed to the story, a fact that would not have surprised Killens at all.

10. There were a few issues missing from the collection at the Schomburg Center for Research in Black Culture. No other articles by Killens appeared in the issues on hand.

11. In letters to literary agent Ronald Hobbs dated January 6, 1968 and January 20, 1968, Julian Mayfield responds to a proposed book project that would deal with issues raised by Cruse's book. Contributors would include himself as well as Julius Lester, John Henrik Clarke, and Killens. The project, however, never came to fruition.

12. Clarke interview by Nuruddin.

13. See Hart, "The Black Aesthetic and the Novels of John Oliver Killens," 74. In a letter to me in 2000, Hart recalled Killens's response when she broached the subject of Cruse during a meeting at Howard University. "It was as if his regard for Cruse was that of a person who is annoyed by a gnat on his arm and who has just to flick the bug away to be done with it!"

CHAPTER 4

1. Killens, "The Half Ain't Never Been Told," 304.

2. In addition to the readings by Hord and Johnson, see Dickson-Carr, *African American Satire*, 142–49.

3. For a fairly elaborate discussion of the veil metaphor, see Gibson, introduction, xi–xv.

4. I have in mind scenes involving the characters Althea Hobbs, Sam Haywood, and the Great Ahmed Khan, which are described in the latter half of the script (90–160).

5. Song of Solomon 1:5.

CHAPTER 5

1. In "Rappin' with Myself" Killens writes, "I come right out of the Old Testament. I believe like Nat Turner, Fred Douglass, Denmark Vesey, Malcolm X, I believe in an eye for an eye, a tooth for a tooth" (106).

2. Killens also reflects Douglass's observation about the imperatives of masters to suppress the aspirations of the enslaved. Like Luke, Douglass heard his master express views about education for the people he owned. Similar to MacKay's admonition that "the moment they stop thinking of themselves as niggers, you're in trouble," Mr. Auld argued that learning and literacy would make slaves unmanageable. See Douglass, Narrative, 29.

3. The Vesey rebellion was originally scheduled to take place July 14, 1822. Because of concerns about security leaks, the date was moved up to June 16. However, the rebels did not strike then because the whites in Charleston seemed to have been tipped off. Subsequently, the movement was infiltrated before the rebellion could be enacted.

4. Killens mentions Lofton's book in his introduction to The Trial Record of Denmark Vesey, vii–xxi. The similar passage from Lofton, Insurrection in South Carolina, reads: "Schooled by long experience as a slave himself and acquainted through his reading with many expressed aspirations for freedom, Vesey had his own opinions as to what the liberties and the rights and privileges of Negroes should be. His notions did not conform to the white views that mere liberation from bondage was the ultimate reward for a black man and that freed slaves should be grateful for small blessings. He was annoyed by the obsequious forms which anyone with dark skin was expected to observe" (132).

5. The lines, as recorded in the novel:

> I will sing of freedom
> And scourge the evil that sits on the throne . . .
> Shudder, pupils of blind fortune
> Tyrants of the world;
> But lend an ear, ye fallen slaves,
> Gain courage and arise!
> It was law, not nature, tyrants,
> Put the crown upon your heads. (114)

6. Pushkin's height is not mentioned by Killens. However, it is noted by Robin Edmonds in *Pushkin*, 132.

CHAPTER 6

1. Arthur Flowers told me this several times between 1997 and 1999 during conversations at Syracuse University.

2. *Freedomways* was published from 1961 to 1985. The word "Negro" was dropped from the subtitle beginning with the summer 1968 issue. For a statement on Killens's role in the founding of the journal, see Jackson, *Freedomways Reader*, xxii, 335. Cruse acknowledges that members of the Harlem Writers Guild were the central figures of *Freedomways*. See *The Crisis of the Negro Intellectual*, 247. Not surprisingly, the longest book review *Freedomways* ever featured was Ernest Kaiser's of *Negro Intellectual*. Killens himself did not contribute much to *Freedomways*, only tributes to Lorraine Hansberry ("Lorraine Hansberry") and Charles White ("He Took His Art More Seriously Than He Did Himself"), and a two-part story "Run Like Hell and Holler Fire!"

3. Although reviewed in *Freedomways*, Killens received no free pass in terms of criticism. John Clarke's review of *And Then We Heard the Thunder* was enthusiastic, and John Henry Jones's review of *'Sippi* was even more favorable. But lukewarm at best were reviews by Earl Durham of *Black Man's Burden*, and by Jean Carey Bond of *The Cotillion*.

4. Under the directorship of Elizabeth Nuñez, who was coordinator for the 1986 event, subsequent conferences were held in 1988, 1991, 1996, and 2000. Participants included Houston Baker, Jr., Amiri Baraka, Gwendolyn Brooks, Henry Louis Gates, Jr., Charles Johnson, Terry McMillan, Haki Madhubuti, Walter Mosley, Arnold Rampersad, Ishmael Reed, Sonia Sanchez, Ntozake Shange, Derek Walcott, Alice Walker, and John Edgar Wideman.

5. Madhubuti founded the Gwendolyn Brooks Writers Conference, which is annually sponsored by the Gwendolyn Brooks Center at Chicago State University.

6. All these authors were members of the Harlem Writers Guild and/or members of a second group cofounded by Killens, the Association of Artists for Freedom.

7. Killens would never supply a ringing endorsement of Ellison's work. But in *Black Man's Burden* he remarks that "a puny achievement is what Ellison's novel was not" (30). In "The Smoking Sixties," he noted, "We waited with great expectations for the second novel of Ralph Ellison, author of the powerful *Invisible Man*" (xvii).

8. Killens, *Black Man's Burden*, 45; Malcolm X, "Statement of Basic Aims
and Objectives of the Organization of Afro-American Unity," 563.

9. Unless otherwise indicated, quotations from the 1986 conference were
transcribed from tapes.

10. As reported by Fuller, Gilman's specific charge was "Negro playwrighting,
as I see it thus far, is in a preliminary stage. It could not be otherwise. It is in
the stage of being an arm of Negro awakening, of Negro political action, of
Negro insistence, not on rights, but on being. Yet drama, as an art, cannot be
concerned with an insistence on the right to be, but on the nature of being.
In this, it is totally democratic and totally aristocratic. Any white dramatist is
compelled to place his head under the guillotine when he writes, and it will fall
off if what he writes is untrue—untrue, need I say, in aesthetic terms." Fuller's
response:

> Negro writers *are*, just as Negroes *are*, and they accept their own being.
> It is not the Negro writer insisting on "the right to be" but the white
> critic who, because of his very special attitude and relationship *vis-à-vis*
> Negroes, visualizes the Negro as struggling to *become*—and *become*, in
> all probability, like white people. It is Mr. Gilman, the white critic,
> who imagines that Negroes are insisting on "the right to be." But the
> truth is that Negro writers have no doubts at all about their "right to
> be"; they are describing in their work "the nature of being," the nature
> of *their* being, the nature of being as reflected through their eyes and
> through their experience, which is all any writer ever does.
>
> And what Mr. Gilman has done—what many white critics
> invariably do—is to pass judgment on the quality of the *being* of
> Negro writers. He has said, in effect, that because Negro writers are
> involved in the struggle against those forces in the society which tend
> to dehumanize their *being* they, therefore, lack the maturity and the
> artistry to produce drama which is also art. The "nature of being" as
> Negro playwrights must see it, Mr. Gilman has implied, inhibits their
> creating a work of art. And then, to heap insult upon his wild, slashing
> wound, Mr. Gilman declared that the best play about Negroes ever
> written was the work not of a Negro but of the Frenchman Jean Genet,
> *The Blacks*, a fantastic pageant of masks and symbols which no Negro
> anywhere in the world could accept as having relevance to his life in
> strictly human terms. (82)

11. In the 1949 essay, Redding argued, for example, that Dunbar in his
short stories succumbed to depicting simplistic characters. He saw Chesnutt
as overriding stereotypes in *The Colonel's Dream* and the *Marrow of Tradition*,
which, in Redding's view, is why Chesnutt was ignored by many readers in

his day. For Redding, examples of works with artistic integrity that were also successful appeals to Black and white audiences were Richard Wright's *Uncle Tom's Children* and *Native Son*, Chester Himes's *If He Hollers Let Him Go* and *Lonely Crusade*, Margaret Walker's *For My People*, Willard Motley's *Knock on Any Door*, and Frank Yerby's *The Foxes of Harrow*, *The Vixens*, and *The Golden Hawk*.

12. For further comments on Hayden's views and life at Fisk, see Hatcher, *From the Auroral Darkness*, 19–30, 36–40, 76–81. Also note Hayden's own accounts and actions: On April 27, 1965, he submitted a letter of resignation to Fisk president Stephen J. Wright. Explaining his reasons, he wrote, "I have endured the increasingly onerous teaching load you have required of me, hoping that eventually I might have earned the right to a lighter schedule which would have left more time and energy for writing. However, your recent appointment of a Writer in Residence has shown me how ill-founded my hopes were. And it seems to indicate a complete disregard for the work I have done over the years with the Creative Writing course here and for my own achievements as a writer. It augurs ill indeed for my future growth and productivity as a member of the Fisk faculty." Hayden retracted his resignation, perhaps because President Wright explained to him in a letter of June 17, 1965, that the funds designated for the residency carried the stipulation that an outside person be selected. In a letter dated February 15, 1968, Killens invited Hayden to be a part of a panel at the 1968 conference at Fisk, but Hayden did not appear on the program. He resigned permanently from Fisk in 1969. In 1974, he received a letter from Haki Madhubuti inviting him to participate in the 1974 conference at Howard University, but he declined.

13. Dudley Randall considers Tolson and Hayden together, along with Gwendolyn Brooks, in "The Black Aesthetic in the Thirties, Forties, and Fifties," 37–40. Sarah Webster Fabio makes critical remarks about Tolson in "Who Speaks Negro?".

14. Along with Tolson and Hayden, participants in the Festival of Negro Poets, which took place October 19–24, were Langston Hughes, Margaret Walker, Zora Neale Hurston, Sterling Brown, Arna Bontemps, Owen Dodson, and Jacob Reddix. For Tolson's comment on Hayden's reading, see Farnsworth, *Melvin B. Tolson*, 203.

15. Of course, all were not in harmony at Fisk. The report also noted that few faculty members were in attendance and, for the most part, faculty, particularly faculty from the English department, did not receive or greet the guest writers.

16. For a more detailed report, see Kent, *A Life of Gwendolyn Brooks*, 153–230; and Brooks, *Report from Part One*, 83–86.

17. Julian Mayfield Papers, Schomburg Center for Research in Black Culture.

18. To follow the Cruse-Mayfield debate to its conclusion in print, see "Reply on a Black Crisis."

19. A complementary description of the period is found in Kelley, *Yo' Mama's Disfunktional*, 4–7.

20. See Windham, "The Long Distance Runner," 41–42; Peeples, "The Artist as Liberator," 10. For a sharply different perspective, see Hernton, *The Sexual Mountain and Black Women Writers*, especially chapters 1 and 2. Also see Walker's own provocative essays "Coming in from the Cold" and "In the Closet of the Soul" included in her collection *Living by the Word*, 54–68, 78–92.

21. Textual treatment of the "Saint Harriet" line of reasoning is traceable to *Black Man's Burden*, 45–46.

22. See Yette, "Black Hero Dynamics and the White Media."

CONCLUSION

1. The other escapees are LeRoi Jones, Don L. Lee, and Ishmael Reed.

2. The subsequent remarks appeared in slightly different form in Gilyard, "John Oliver Killens."

3. The questions posed were as follows: 1. When the artist, black or white, portrays Negro characters is he under any obligations or limitations as to the sort of character he will portray? 2. Can any author be criticized for painting the worst or the best characters of a group? 3. Can any author be criticized for refusing to handle novels that portray Negroes of education and accomplishment, on the grounds that these characters are no different from white folk and therefore not interesting? 4. What are Negroes to do when they are continually painted at their worst and judged by the public as they are painted? 5. Does the situation of the educated Negro in America with its pathos, humiliation and tragedy call for artistic treatment at least as sincere and sympathetic as "Porgy" received? 6. Is not the continual portrayal of the sordid, foolish criminal among Negroes convincing the world that this and this alone is really and essentially Negroid, and preventing white artists from knowing any other types and preventing black artists from daring to paint them? 7. Is there not a real danger that young colored writers will be tempted to follow the popular trend in portraying Negro character in the underworld rather than seeking to paint the truth about themselves and their own social class?

4. These stories were told to me between 1984 and 1986 at Medgar Evers College.

bibliography

Abernathy, Ralph. *And the Walls Came Tumbling Down*. New York: Harper and Row, 1989.

The American Negro Writer and His Roots: Selected Papers from the First Conference of Negro Writers, March, 1959. New York: American Society of African Culture, 1960.

Angelou, Maya. *The Heart of a Woman*. 1981. Reprint, New York: Bantam Books, 1982.

Baldwin, James. *Another Country*. 1962. Reprint, New York: Dell Books, 1963.

Baraka, Amiri. *Blues People: Negro Music in White America*. New York: William Morrow, 1963.

————. "Poem for Halfwhite College Students." In *Transbluesency: The Selected Poems of Amiri Baraka/LeRoi Jones, Selected Poems 1961–1995*, ed. Paul Vangelisti, 144. New York: Marsilio, 1995.

Basaninyenzi, Gatsinzi. "Ideology and Four Post-1960 Afro-American Novelists." Ph.D. diss., University of Iowa, 1986.

Belafonte, Harry. *Belafonte at Carnegie Hall*. RCA Victor LPC/LSO 6006, 1959.

Bell, Bernard. *The Afro-American Novel and Its Tradition*. Amherst: University of Massachusetts Press, 1987.

Bond, Jean Carey. "'Killens' New Novel a Satire on Black 'Society.'" Review of *The Cotillion; or, One Good Bull Is Half the Herd*, by John Oliver Killens. *Freedomways* (spring 1971): 203–5.

Bontemps, Arna. *Black Thunder*. 1936. Reprint, Boston: Beacon Press, 1992.

Booth, Wayne. *The Rhetoric of Fiction*. 2d ed. Chicago: University of Chicago Press, 1983.

Branch, Taylor. *Pillar of Fire: America in the King Years, 1963–1965*. New York: Simon and Schuster, 1998.

Breen, Deborah. Letter to Keith Gilyard. February 19, 1998.

Breitman, George. *The Last Year of Malcolm X: The Evolution of a Revolutionary*. New York: Pathfinder Press, 1967.

Brooks, Gwendolyn. *Report from Part One*. Detroit: Broadside Press, 1972.

Carey, Stephen Anderson. "Black Men's Du Boisian Relationships to Southern Social Institutions in the Novels of John Oliver Killens." Ph.D. diss., University of Texas at Dallas, 1992.

157

Carmichael, Stokely, and Charles V. Hamilton. *Black Power: The Politics of Liberation in America*. New York: Random House, 1967.

Carson, Clayborne, ed. *The Papers of Martin Luther King, Jr*. Vol. 3. Berkeley: University of California Press, 1997.

———. *The Papers of Martin Luther King, Jr*. Vol. 4. Berkeley: University of California Press, 2000.

Chander, Harish. "John Oliver Killens." In *Contemporary African American Novelists: A Bio-Bibliographical Critical Sourcebook*, ed. Emmanuel S. Nelson, 250–59. Westport, CT: Greenwood Press, 1999.

Chayefsky, Paddy. *Network*. Hollywood: Script City, 1976.

Chesnutt, Charles W. *The Colonel's Dream*. 1905. Reprint, Miami: Mnemosyne Publishing, 1969.

———. *The Marrow of Tradition*. 1901. Reprint, Ann Arbor: Ann Arbor Paperbacks, 1969.

———. "Response to Questionnaire about the Negro in Art." *The Crisis* (November 1926): 28–29.

Clark, Steve. Introduction to *By Any Means Necessary*, by Malcolm X. New York: Pathfinder Press, 1970.

Clarke, John Henrik. "*The Crisis of the Negro Intellectual* by Harold Cruse: A Reappraisal of Some Neglected Aspects of the Crisis." In *Africans at the Crossroads: Notes for an African World Revolution*, 365–81. Trenton: Africa World Press, 1991.

———. " Negro Men at War." Review of *And Then We Heard the Thunder*, by John Oliver Killens. *Freedomways* (spring 1963): 227–29.

———. Review of *Youngblood*. *Freedom* (August 1954): 7.

Clarke, John Henrik, ed. *William Styron's Nat Turner: Ten Black Writers Respond*. Boston: Beacon Press, 1968.

Cohen, Norm. *Long Steel Rail*. Urbana: University of Illinois Press, 1981.

Cone, James. *The Spirituals and the Blues: An Interpretation*. Maryknoll, NY: Orbis Books, 1992.

"On the Conference Beat." *Negro Digest* (March 1967): 90–93.

Corbett, Edward, and Robert Conners, eds. *Classical Rhetoric for the Modern Student*. 4th ed. New York: Oxford University Press, 1999.

Cruse, Harold. *The Crisis of the Negro Intellectual: A Historical Analysis of the Failure of Black Leadership*. 1967. Reprint, New York: Quill, 1984.

———. "Reply on a Black Crisis." *Negro Digest* (November 1968): 19–25, 65–69.

Dickson-Carr, Daryl. *African American Satire: The Sacredly Profane Novel*. Columbia: University of Missouri Press, 2001.

Douglass, Frederick. *Narrative of the Life of Frederick Douglass, An American Slave, Written by Himself*. 1845. Reprint, New York: W. W. Norton, 1997.

————. "The Significance of Emancipation in the West Indies: An Address Delivered in Canandaigua, New York, on 3 August 1857." In *The Frederick Douglass Papers, Series One: Speeches, Debates, and Interviews, Volume 3: 1855–63*, ed. John Blassingame, 183–208. New Haven: Yale University Press, 1985.

Dubey, Madhu. *Black Women Novelists and the Nationalist Aesthetic*. Bloomington: Indiana University Press, 1994.

Du Bois, W. E. B. "Criteria of Negro Art." *The Crisis* (October 1926): 290–97.

————. *The Souls of Black Folk*. 1903. Reprint, New York: Penguin, 1989.

————. "The Talented Tenth." 1903. In *The Future of the Race*, ed. Henry Louis Gates, Jr., and Cornel West, 133–57. New York: Knopf, 1996.

————. "The Talented Tenth Memorial Address." 1948. In *The Future of the Race*, ed. Henry Louis Gates, Jr., and Cornel West, 159–77. New York: Knopf, 1996.

Durham, Earl. "Capturing the Negro Mood." Review of *Black Man's Burden*, by John Oliver Killens. *Freedomways* (spring 1966): 182–84.

Dyson, Michael Eric. *Making Malcolm: The Myth and Meaning of Malcolm X*. New York: Oxford University Press, 1995.

Echewa, Thomas. "Africans vs. Afro-Americans." *Negro Digest* (January 1965): 33–38.

————. "Reply to an American Negro." *Negro Digest* (September 1965): 23–27.

Edmonds, Robin. *Pushkin: The Man and His Age*. New York: St Martin's Press, 1994.

Ellison, Ralph. *Invisible Man*. New York: Random House, 1952.

Evans, Mari. "Speak the Truth to the People." In *Call & Response: The Riverside Anthology of the African American Literary Tradition*, ed. Patricia Liggins Hill, Bernard Bell, Trudier Harris, William J. Harris, R. Baxter Miller, and Sandra O'Neale, 1575–76. Boston: Houghton Mifflin, 1998.

Fabio, Sarah Webster. "Tripping with Black Writing." 1971. In *Within the Circle: An Anthology of African American Literary Criticism from the Harlem Renaissance to the Present*, ed. Angelyn Mitchell, 224–31. Durham: Duke University Press, 1994.

————. "Who Speaks Negro?" *Negro Digest* (1966): 54–58.

Farnsworth, Robert. *Melvin B. Tolson, 1898–1966: Plain Talk and Poetic Prophecy*. Columbia: University of Missouri Press, 1984.

Faucet, Jessie. "Response to Questionnaire about the Negro in Art." *The Crisis* (June 1926): 71–72.

Faulkner, William. "A Letter to the North." *Life*, March 5 1956, pp. 51–52.

Finnegan, Ruth. *Limba Stories and Story-Telling*. Oxford: Oxford University Press, 1967.

Fuller, Hoyt. "Reverberations from a Writers' Conference." *African Forum* 1, no. 2 (1965): 78–84.

———. "Towards a Black Aesthetic." 1968. In *Within the Circle: An Anthology of African American Literary Criticism from the Harlem Renaissance to the Present,* ed. Angelyn Mitchell, 199–206. Durham: Duke University Press, 1994.

Gaines, Ernest. *The Autobiography of Miss Jane Pittman.* 1971. Reprint, New York: Bantam Books, 1972.

———. *Of Love and Dust.* 1967. Reprint, New York: Bantam Books, 1969.

Gates, Henry Louis, Jr., and Nellie McKay, eds. *The Norton Anthology of African American Literature.* New York: W. W. Norton, 1997.

Gayle, Addison. Introduction to *Great Black Russian,* by John Oliver Killens. Detroit: Wayne State University Press, 1989.

———. *The Way of the New World: The Black Novel in America.* Garden City, NY: Doubleday, 1975.

Gerould, Gordon Hall. *The Ballad of Tradition.* Oxford: Oxford University Press, 1932.

Gibson, Donald. Introduction to *The Souls of Black Folk,* by W. E. B. Du Bois. New York: Penguin, 1989.

Gilyard, Keith. "Genopsycholinguisticide and the Language Theme in African American Fiction." *College English* 52 (1990): 776–86.

———. "John Oliver Killens." In *The Before Columbus Foundation Fiction Anthology: Selections from the American Book Awards 1980–1990,* ed. Ishmael Reed, Kathryn Trueblood, and Shawn Wong, 389–91. New York: W. W. Norton, 1992.

Guy, Rosa. *Bird at My Window.* Philadelphia: J. B. Lippincott, 1966.

Hampton, Henry, and Steve Fayer, eds. *Voices of Freedom: An Oral History of the Civil Rights Movement from the 1950s through the 1980s.* New York: Bantam Books, 1990.

Handler, M. S. "2 Negro Writers Open Talk Series." *New York Times,* April 25, 1965, p. 31.

Harris, Norman. "Understanding the Sixties: A Study of Character Development and Theme in Seven Recent Afro-American Novels." Ph.D. diss., Indiana University, 1980.

Hart, Betty. "The Black Aesthetic and the Novels of John Oliver Killens." Master's thesis, West Virginia University, 1974.

Hatch, Gary Lane. *Arguing in Communities.* Mountain View, CA: Mayfield, 1996.

Hatcher, John. *From the Auroral Darkness: The Life and Poetry of Robert Hayden.* Oxford: George Ronald, 1984.

Hayden, Robert. "Frederick Douglass." In *Collected Poems.* New York: Liveright, 1985.

————. Letter to Stephen J. Wright. April 25, 1965. Robert Hayden papers, National Baha'i Archives.

————. "Homage to the Empress of the Blues." In *Collected Poems*. New York: Liveright, 1985.

————. "Middle Passage." In *Collected Poems*. New York: Liveright, 1985.

————. "Runagate Runagate." In *Collected Poems*. New York: Liveright, 1985.

Hayden, Robert, ed. *Kaleidoscope: Poems by American Negro Poets*. New York: Harcourt, Brace and World, 1967.

Henderson, Stephen. *Understanding the New Black Poetry: Black Music and Black Speech as Poetic References*. New York: William Morrow, 1973.

Hernton, Calvin. *The Sexual Mountain and Black Women Writers*. New York: Doubleday, 1987.

Hill, Patricia Liggins, Bernard Bell, Trudier Harris, William J. Harris, R. Baxter Miller, and Sandra O'Neale, eds. *Call & Response: The Riverside Anthology of the African American Literary Tradition*. Boston: Houghton Mifflin, 1998.

Himes, Chester. *If He Hollers Let Him Go*. 1945. Reprint, New York: Signet, 1971.

————. *Lonely Crusade*. 1949. Reprint, Chatham, NJ: Chatham Bookseller, 1973.

Hord, Fred Lee. *Reconstructing Memory: Black Literary Criticism*. Chicago: Third World Press, 1991.

Howard-Pitney, David. *The Afro-American Jeremiad: Appeals for Justice in America*. Philadelphia: Temple University Press, 1990.

Howe, Russell. "New Civil War If Negro Claims Are Pressed: An Exclusive Interview with William Faulkner." London *Sunday Times*, March 4, 1956, p. 7.

Hughes, Langston. *Famous American Negroes*. New York: Dodd, Mead, 1954.

————. "Mother to Son." In *The Collected Poems of Langston Hughes*, ed. Arnold Rampersad and David Roessel, 30. New York: Vintage, 1995.

————. "The Negro Mother." In *The Collected Poems of Langston Hughes*, ed. Arnold Rampersad and David Roessel, 155–56. New York: Vintage, 1995.

Jackson, Esther Cooper, ed. *Freedomways Reader: Prophets in Their Own Country*. Boulder, CO: Westview Press, 2000.

Jay-Z. "I Just Wanna Love U (Give It to Me)." *The Dynasty: Roc La Familia*. Polygram Records, 2000. ASIN: B000050HS9.

Johnson, Charles. *Being & Race: Black Writing since 1970*. Bloomington: Indiana University Press, 1988.

Johnson, Georgia Douglas. "Response to Questionnaire about the Negro in Art." *The Crisis* (August 1926): 193.

Jones, Gayl. *Liberating Voices: Oral Tradition in African American Literature*. 1991. Reprint, New York: Penguin, 1992.

Jones, John Henry. "Killens' Fine, Sensitive New Novel" Review of *'Sippi*. *Freedomways* (fall 1967): 373–75.

Jones, LeRoi. See Amiri Baraka.

Kaiser, Ernest. Review of *The Crisis of the Negro Intellectual*. *Freedomways* (winter 1969): 24–41.

Keats, Ezra Jack. *John Henry: An American Legend*. New York: Pantheon, 1965.

Kelley, Robin D. G. *Yo' Mama's Disfunktional: Fighting the Culture Wars in Urban America*. Boston: Beacon Press, 1997.

Kelley, William Melvin. *A Different Drummer*. 1962. Reprint, New York: Anchor Books, 1989.

———. *Dunsfords Travels Everywhere*. Garden City, NY: Doubleday, 1970.

Kent, George. *A Life of Gwendolyn Brooks*. Lexington: University Press of Kentucky, 1990.

Killens, John Oliver. *And Then We Heard the Thunder*. 1962. Reprint, Washington, DC: Howard University Press, 1983.

———. "An Appreciation." In *This Child's Gonna Live*, by Sarah Wright. New York: Feminist Press at City University of New York, 1986.

———. "The Artist and the Black University." *The Black Scholar* (November 1969): 61–65.

———. "The Black Culture Generation Gap." *Black World* (August 1973): 22–33.

———. "Black Labor and the Liberation Movement." *The Black Scholar* (October 1970): 33–39.

———. *Black Man's Burden*. New York: Trident Press, 1965.

———. "The Black Writer and the Revolution." *Arts and Society* 5 (1968): 395–99.

———. "Broadway in Black and White." *African Forum* 1, no. 3 (1966): 66–76.

———. "Brotherhood of Blackness." *Negro Digest* (May 1966): 4–10.

———. "The Confessions of Willie Styron." In *William Styron's Nat Turner: Ten Black Writers Respond*, ed. John Henrik Clarke, 34–44. Boston: Beacon Press, 1968.

———. *The Cotillion; or, One Good Bull Is Half the Herd*. New York: Trident Press, 1971.

———. "God Bless America." 1952. In *Black American Stories: A Century of the Best*, ed. Langston Hughes, 204–9. New York: Hill and Wang, 1966.

———. "A Good Man Feeling Bad!" *The Urbanite* (March 1961): 22–24.

———. *Great Black Russian: A Novel on the Life and Times of Alexander Pushkin*. Detroit: Wayne State University Press, 1989.

———. *Great Gittin' Up Morning: The Story of Denmark Vesey*. Garden City, NY: Doubleday, 1972.

————. "The Half Ain't Never Been Told." In *Contemporary Authors Autobi-ography Series*, Vol. 2. Ed. Adele Sarkissian, 279–306. Detroit: Gale, 1985.

————. "He Took His Art More Seriously Than He Did Himself." *Freedomways* (summer 1980): 192–94.

————. "Hollywood in Black and White." In *White Racism: Its History, Pathol-ogy and Practice*, ed. Barry Schwartz and Robert Disch, 398–407. New York: Dell, 1970.

————. "The Image of Black Folk in American Literature." *The Black Scholar* (June 1975): 44–52.

————. Introduction to *An ABC of Color*, by W. E. B. Du Bois. New York: International Publishers, 1969.

————. Introduction to *Black Southern Voices: An Anthology of Fiction, Poetry, Drama, Nonfiction, and Critical Essays*, ed. John Oliver Killens and Jerry Ward, Jr. New York: Meridian, 1992.

————. Letter to Julian Mayfield. Jan. 16, 1968. Julian Mayfield Papers, Schom-burg Center for Research in Black Culture.

————. Letter to Robert Hayden. February 15, 1968. Robert Hayden Papers, National Baha'i Archives.

————. "Lorraine Hansberry: On Time!" *Freedomways* (fall 1979): 273–76.

————. *A Man Ain't Nothin' but a Man: The Adventures of John Henry*. Boston: Little, Brown, 1975.

————. "The Negro as Music Maker: Some Reflections on the Origins of Jazz." *The Urbanite* (April 1961): 7, 29, 33.

————. "Opportunities for Development of Negro Talent." *The American Negro Writer and His Roots: Selected Papers from the First Conference of Negro Writers March, 1959*. New York: American Society of African Culture, 1960.

————. "Rappin' with Myself." In *Amistad 2: Writings on Black History and Culture*, ed. John A. Williams and Charles Harris, 97–136. New York: Vintage Books, 1971.

————. "Reflections from a Black Notebook." *Black Creation* (April 1971): 12–14.

————. Review of *Invisible Man. Freedom* (June 1952): 7.

————. "Rough Diamond." In *Harlem: Voices from the Soul of Black America*, ed. John Henrik Clarke, 169–84. New York: Signet, 1970.

————. "Run Like Hell and Holler Fire!" *Freedomways* (fall 1983): 244–56, (fall 1984): 260–66.

————. *'Sippi*. 1967. Reprint, New York: Thunder's Mouth Press, 1988.

————. *Slaves*. New York: Pyramid, 1969.

————. "The Smoking Sixties." In *Black Short Story Anthology*, ed. Woodie King, Jr., xi–xviii. New York: Columbia University Press, 1972.

————. "Wanted: Some Black Long Distance Runners." *The Black Scholar* (November 1973): 2–7.

————. *Youngblood*. 1954. Reprint, Athens: University of Georgia Press, 1982.

————, ed. *The Trial Record of Denmark Vesey*. Boston: Beacon Press, 1970.

King, Coretta Scott. *My Life with Martin Luther King, Jr*. 1969. Reprint, New York: Penguin, 1993.

King, Martin Luther, Jr. "Letter from Birmingham Jail." 1963. In *The Norton Anthology of African American Literature*, ed. Henry Louis Gates, Jr., and Nellie McKay, 1854–66. New York: W. W. Norton, 1997.

————. *Where Do We Go from Here? Chaos or Community?* 1967. Reprint, Boston: Beacon Press, 1968.

Kipling, Rudyard. "Gunga Din." In *Rudyard Kipling: The Complete Verse*. London: Kyle Cathie Limited, 1990.

Knopf, Alfred. "Response to Questionnaire about the Negro in Art." *The Crisis* (April 1926): 280.

Lee, Don L. See Haki Madhubuti.

Lehman, Paul Robert. "The Development of a Black Psyche in the Works of John Oliver Killens." Ph.D. diss., Lehigh University, 1976.

Llorens, David. "Writers Converge at Fisk University." *Negro Digest* (June 1966): 54–68.

Lofton, John. *Insurrection in South Carolina: The Turbulent World of Denmark Vesey*. Yellow Springs, OH: Antioch Press, 1964.

Lukács, Georg. *Realism in Our Time: Literature and the Class Struggle*. 1963. Reprint, New York: Harper Torchbooks, 1971.

McDowell, Deborah. "Boundaries: Or Distant Relations and Close Kin." In *Afro-American Literary Study in the 1990's*, ed. Houston A. Baker, Jr. and Patricia Redmond, 51–77. Chicago: University of Chicago Press, 1989.

McKay, Claude. *Banana Bottom*. 1933. Reprint, New York: Harvest Books, 1970.

Macon, Wanda. "John O. Killens." *The Oxford Companion to African American Literature*, ed. William Andrews, Frances Smith Foster, and Trudier Harris, 419–20. New York: Oxford University Press, 1997.

Madhubuti, Haki. "But He Was Cool, or: He Even Stopped for Green Lights." In *GroundWork: New and Selected Poems of Don L. Lee/Haki R. Madhubuti from 1966–1996*. Chicago: Third World Press, 1996.

————. "The New Integrationist." In *GroundWork: New and Selected Poems of Don L. Lee/Haki R. Madhubuti from 1966–1996*. Chicago: Third World Press, 1996.

Magill, Frank, ed. *Masterpieces of African-American Literature*. New York: HarperCollins, 1992.

Malcolm X. "Basic Unity Program, Organization of Afro-American Unity." In *New Black Voices: An Anthology of Contemporary Afro-American Literature*, ed. Abraham Chapman, 564–74. New York: Mentor, 1972.

————. By Any Means Necessary. New York: Pathfinder Press, 1970.

————. "Statement of Basic Aims and Objectives of the Organization of Afro-American Unity." 1964. In New Black Voices: An Anthology of Contemporary Afro-American Literature, ed. Abraham Chapman, 558–64. New York: Mentor, 1972.

Mayfield, Julian. "Crisis or Crusade?" Negro Digest (June 1968): 10–24.

————. "Julian Mayfield's Response to Harold Cruse." Negro Digest (November 1968): 26–27.

————. Letter to Ronald Hobbs. Jan 6 1968. Julian Mayfield Papers, Schomburg Center for Research in Black Culture.

————. Letter to Ronald Hobbs. Jan 20, 1968. Julian Mayfield Papers, Schomburg Center for Research in Black Culture.

"The Meaning and Measure of Black Power." Negro Digest (November 1966): 20–37, 81–96.

Mencken, H. L. "Response to Questionnaire about the Negro in Art." The Crisis (March 1926): 219–20.

Miller, Keith. "Martin Luther King, Jr. Borrows a Revolution." College English 48 (1986): 249–65.

Morgan, Marcyliena. " 'Nuthin' but a G Thang': Grammar and Language Ideology in Hip Hop Identity." In Sociocultural and Historical Contexts of African American English, ed. Sonja L. Lanehart, 187–209. Amsterdam: John Benjamins, 2001.

Morrison, Toni. Beloved. New York: Knopf, 1987.

————. The Bluest Eye. New York: Knopf, 1970.

Motley, Willard. Knock on Any Door. 1947. Reprint, New York: Signet, 1950.

Neal, Larry. "And Shine Swam On." In Black Fire: An Anthology of Afro-American Writing, ed. LeRoi Jones and Larry Neal, 638–56. New York: William Morrow, 1968.

————. "The Black Arts Movement." 1968. In Within the Circle: An Anthology of African American Literary Criticism from the Harlem Renaissance to the Present, ed. Angelyn Mitchell, 184–98. Durham: Duke University Press, 1994.

Newman, Richard. Go Down, Moses: Celebrating the African-American Spiritual. New York: Clarkson Potter, 1998.

Nikola-Lisa, W. "John Henry: Then and Now." African American Review (spring 1998): 51–56.

The Notorious B.I.G. "The World Is Filled." Life after Death. Bad Boy Records. 78612–73011-2, 1997.

Onstott, Kyle. Mandingo. Richmond, VA: Delinger, 1957.

Paine, Thomas. American Crisis. 1776. In The Heath Anthology of American Literature Third Edition. Vol. 1. Ed. Paul Lauter. Boston: Houghton Mifflin, 1998.

Parks, Carole A. "The National Black Writers Convention." *Black World* (January 1975): 86–92.

Peeples, Kenneth, Jr. "The Artist as Liberator: An Interview with John Oliver Killens." *Community Review* (fall 1984): 6–14.

Peterson, Bernard, Jr. "John Oliver Killens." In *Contemporary Black American Playwrights and Their Plays: A Biographical Directory and Dramatic Index.* New York: Greenwood Press, 1988.

"Questionnaire about the Negro in Art." *The Crisis* (February 1926): 165.

Rampersad, Arnold. *The Life of Langston Hughes.* Vol. 1: 1902–1941. Oxford: Oxford University Press, 1986.

Randall, Dudley. "The Black Aesthetic in the Thirties, Forties, and Fifties." In *Modern Black Poets: A Collection of Critical Essays*, ed. Donald Gibson, 34–42. Englewood, NJ: Prentice Hall, 1973.

Randolph, A. Philip, and Chandler Owen. "The Steel Drivin' Man." 1925. In *African American Literature*, ed. Demetrice Worley and Jesse Perry, Jr., 73–75. Lincolnwood, IL: National Textbook Company, 1993.

Redding, J. Saunders. "American Negro Literature." *The American Scholar* (spring 1949): 137–48.

———. "The Negro Author: His Publisher, His Public and His Purse." 1945. In *A Scholar's Conscience: Selected Writings of J. Saunders Redding 1942–1977*, ed. Faith Berry, 140–46. Lexington: University Press of Kentucky, 1992.

———. "The Negro Writer and His Relationship to His Roots." In *The American Negro Writer and His Roots: Selected Papers from the First Conference of Negro Writers March, 1959.* New York: American Society of African Culture, 1960.

———. Review of *Bird at My Window. The Crisis* (April 1966): 225, 227.

Review of *Slaves. Publishers Weekly*, April 14, 1969, p. 99.

Shange, Ntozake. *for colored girls who have considered suicide/when the rainbow is enuf.* 1975. Reprint, New York: Scribner, 1997.

Smith, Rochelle, and Sharon Jones, eds. *The Prentice Hall Anthology of African American Literature.* Upper Saddle River, NJ: Prentice Hall, 2000.

Smitherman, Geneva. *Black Talk: Words and Phrases from the Hood to the Amen Corner.* Boston: Houghton Mifflin, 1994.

———. *Talkin and Testifyin: The Language of Black America.* Boston: Houghton Mifflin, 1977.

Spalding, Henry, ed. *Encyclopedia of Black Folklore and Humor.* New York: Jonathan David Publishers, 1972.

Stowe, Harriet Beecher. *Uncle Tom's Cabin.* 1852. Reprint, Columbus, OH: Charles E. Merrill, 1969.

Styron, William. *The Confessions of Nat Turner.* New York: Random House, 1967.

Talese, Gay. "Many Words, Mostly Hot, Mark Writers' Parley." *New York Times*, April 26, 1965, p. 26.

"The Task of the Negro Writer as Artist: A Symposium." *Negro Digest* (April 1965): 54–70, 72–83.

Thurman, Wallace. *Blacker the Berry: A Novel of Negro Life*. 1929. Reprint, New York: Collier Books, 1970.

Van Vechten, Carl. "Response to Questionnaire about the Negro in Art." *The Crisis* (March 1926): 219.

Vincent, Theodore. *Black Power and the Garvey Movement*. San Francisco: Ramparts Press, 1972.

Walker, Alice. *The Color Purple*. San Diego: Harcourt Brace Jovanovich, 1982.

———. *Living by the Word: Selected Writings 1973–1987*. San Diego: Harcourt Brace Jovanovich, 1989.

Walker, Margaret. "For My People." 1937. In *The Norton Anthology of African American Literature*, ed. Henry Louis Gates, Jr., and Nellie McKay, 1572–73. New York: W. W. Norton, 1997.

Welty, Eudora. *One Writer's Beginnings*. 1983. Reprint, New York: Warner, 1985.

White, Walter. "Response to Questionnaire about the Negro in Art." *The Crisis* (April 1926): 279–80.

Wiggins, William, Jr. "The Structure and Dynamics of Folklore in the Novel Form: The Case of John O. Killens." *Keystone Folklore Quarterly* (fall 1972): 92–117.

Williams, Brett. *John Henry: A Bio-Bibliography*. Westport, CT: Greenwood Press, 1983.

Williams, John A. *Captain Blackman*. 1972. Reprint, New York: Bantam Books, 1974.

———. *The Man Who Cried I Am*. 1967. Reprint, New York: Signet, 1968.

———. *Night Song*. 1961. Reprint, New York: Pocket Books, 1970.

———. "Open Letter to an African." *Negro Digest* (September 1965): 22, 28–35.

Windham, Revish. "The Long Distance Runner: An Interview with John Oliver Killens." *Black Forum* (fall/winter 1978): 4–7, 28–31, 40–43.

Wright, Richard. *12 Million Black Voices: A Folk History of the Negro in the United States*. 1941. Richard Wright Reader. New York: Da Capo Press, 1997.

———. *Black Boy: A Record of Childhood and Youth*. New York: Harper, 1945.

———. "The Ethics of Living Jim Crow: An Autobiographical Sketch." 1937. In *Richard Wright: Early Works*, 225–37. New York: Library of America, 1991.

———. *Native Son*. New York: Harper and Brothers, 1940.

———. *Uncle Tom's Children*. New York: Harper and Brothers, 1938.

Wright, Stephen J. Letter to Robert Hayden. June 17, 1965. Robert Hayden
    Papers, National Baha'i Archives.
Yarmolinsky, Avrahm, ed. *The Poems, Prose and Plays of Alexander Pushkin*. New
    York: Random House, 1936/1964.
Yerby, Frank. *The Foxes of Harrow*. New York: Dial, 1946.
———. *The Vixens*. 1947. Reprint, New York: Pocket Books, 1965.
———. *The Golden Hawk*. 1948. Reprint, New York: Dell Books, 1982.
Yette, Samuel. "Black Hero Dynamics and the White Media." *Black World*
    (January 1975): 22–28.

index

Abernathy, Ralph, 149n. 6
Abstentionism, 59
Accomodationism, 43, 47
Activism. *See* Politics/activism
Africa, 81, 82
African Americans: and Black Arts
    Movement, 3; and cultural infe-
    riority, 85; and identity, 82; and
    jeremiad, 63; and Malcolm X,
    64; and self-esteem, 67, 93; and
    Youngblood, 17, 18, 20, 21–22.
    See also Blackness; Black Power
"Africans *vs.* Afro-Americans"
    (Echewa), 69
Afro-Americanese. *See* Vernacular
*Afro-American Novel and Its Tradition,
    The* (Bell), 47, 48
Amen Corner, 57, 148n. 10
"American Negro Literature"
    (Redding), 120
"American Negro Writer and His
    Roots, The" (American Society
    of African Culture conference),
    115
American Society of African Culture,
    115, 116, 120
AMSAC. *See* American Society of
    African Culture
And Then We Heard the Thunder
    (Killens), 37–57, 61, 63, 75, 139,
    141, 142

Angelou, Maya, 135; *Heart of A
    Woman*, 46
Aptheker, Herbert, 116, 117
Art, 3, 9, 10, 26, 79, 117, 121, 136,
    137, 140, 142, 155n. 3. *See also*
    Black Aesthetic; Black Arts
    Movement; Writers/writing
Audience, 64, 75, 121, 122, 140

Baines, Myrna, 117
Baldwin, James, 117–18, 120, 124,
    133
Ballad, 32, 103, 145n. 16
Ballard Normal School, 18
Bambara, Toni Cade, 135–36
Baraka, Amiri, 92, 119, 123, 126,
    136–37, 145n. 16
Basaninyenzi, Gatsinzi, 43; "Ideology
    and Four Post-1960 Afro-
    American Novelists," 39, 40
Beauty, 93
Being & Race (Johnson), 84
Belafonte, Harry, 106, 107–8
Bell, Bernard, 2, 147n. 4; *The Afro-
    American Novel and Its Tradition*,
    47, 48
Bennett, Lerone, 123, 124, 125
Bennett, Mrs., 99
Bible, 27, 54, 89–90, 97, 98, 101, 102,
    103, 151n. 1
Big Mama, 11, 14

OAAU. *See* Organization of Afro-
American Unity
One Writer's Beginnings (Welty), 26
Operation Dixie, 20
Orality, 5, 32. *See also* Language
Organization of Afro-American
Unity, 5, 59, 70, 75, 148n. 1,
148nn. 1, 3
Owen, Chandler, 104

Pan-Africanism, 69, 130, 146n. 21
Parallelism, 32, 145n. 15
Parataxis, 32, 145n. 15
Parks, Carole A., 131
Patterson, Mrs. Priscilla, 80, 84
Peeples, Kenneth, 109
Perkins, Eugene, 131
Pluralism, 25
Politics/activism: and *And Then We
Heard the Thunder*, 37, 43; and
Baraka, 137; and conferences,
4; and *The Cotillion*, 82, 89; and
Hayden, 121; and images, 131;
and Killens's style, 1, 2; and *A
Man Ain't Nothin' but a Man*,
105; and *'Sippi*, 9, 23, 25; and
writers, 141; and *Youngblood*, 9
Power, 6
Prison, 136
Progressivism, 25
Propaganda, 2, 3, 10, 121, 142.
See also Art; Politics/activism;
Writers/writing
Prosser, Gabriel, 69
Pryor, Richard, 129
Psychology, 2, 42–43, 54, 95, 139
Purdy, Reverend, 22, 23–24, 32
Pushkin, Alexander, 107–8, 109–11,
139
Pushkin, Alexander (character),
108–9, 111

Race/ethnicity, 26, 63, 104, 105, 106
Racism, 11, 14, 37, 44, 133
Raglin, Ida Mae, 22
Rakestraw, Cora Mae, 22
Randall, Dudley, 126
Randolph, A. Philip, 104
"Rappin' with Myself" (Killens),
49–50, 77, 123, 140, 142, 151n.
1
Realism, 2, 22, 47, 91
Rebellion: and Cruse, 70; and *Great
Black Russian*, 108; and *Great
Gittin' Up Morning*, 100–103;
and Malcolm X, 59; optimism
about, 128–29; and Organization
of Afro-American Unity, 60;
and Pushkin, 111; and *'Sippi*,
22, 29, 31; and *Slaves*, 97, 99;
and *And Then We Heard the
Thunder* (Killens), 47; and Vesey,
151nn. 1, 3, 4; and writers,
79; and *Youngblood*, 13, 27.
See also Liberation/freedom;
Riot
Reconstructing Memory (Hord), 84
Redding, J. Saunders, 153n. 11;
"American Negro Literature,"
120; "The Negro Author: His
Publisher, His Public and His
Purse," 120; "The Negro Writer
and His Relationship to His
Roots," 120
"Reflections from a Black Notebook"
(Killens), 39, 42
Reform, 70
Religion, 53–54, 89–90, 97, 98, 101–2
Repetition, 32
Resistance. *See* Rebellion
"Reverberations from a Writers
Conference" (Fuller), 119
Revolution. *See* Rebellion

Books in the African American Life Series

African Americans, edited by James Oliver Horton and Lois E. Horton, 1997 (reprint)

Tell It to Women: An Epic Drama for Women, by Osonye Tess Onwueme, 1997

Ed Bullins: A Literary Biography, by Samuel Hay, 1997

Walkin' over Medicine, by Loudelle F. Snow, 1998 (reprint)

Negroes with Guns, by Robert F. Williams, 1998 (reprint)

A Study of Walter Rodney's Intellectual and Political Thought, by Rupert Lewis, 1998

Ideology and Change: The Transformation of the Caribbean Left, by Perry Mars, 1998

"Winds Can Wake Up the Dead": An Eric Walrond Reader, edited by Louis Parascandola, 1998

Race & Ideology: Language, Symbolism, and Popular Culture, edited by Arthur Spears, 1999

Without Hatreds or Fears: Jorge Artel and the Struggle for Black Literary Expression in Colombia, by Laurence E. Prescott, 2000

African Americans, Labor, and Society: Organizing for a New Agenda, edited by Patrick L. Mason, 2001

The Concept of Self: A Study of Black Identity and Self-Esteem, by Richard L. Allen, 2001

What the Wine-Sellers Buy Plus Three: Four Plays by Ron Milner, 2001

Looking Within/Mirar adentro: Selected Poems, 1954–2000 by Nancy Morejón, 2003

Liberation Memories: The Rhetoric and Poetics of John Oliver Killens, by Keith Gilyard, 2003

For an updated listing of books in this series, please visit our Web site at http://wsupress.wayne.edu

www.ingramcontent.com/pod-product-compliance
Lightning Source LLC
Chambersburg PA
CBHW070438100426
42812CB00031B/3328/J